The Administration of Company Meetings

A PRACTICAL GUIDE

Dennis Roberts, B.Sc.(Econ.), FCIS

Past President of
The Institute of Chartered Secretaries and Administrators

ICSA Publishing · Cambridge

Published by ICSA Publishing Ltd
Fitzwilliam House, 32 Trumpington Street, Cambridge CB2 1QY, England
and
27 South Main Street, Wolfeboro, New Hampshire, 03894–2069, USA

First published 1986

British Library Cataloguing in Publication Data
Roberts, Dennis
The administration of company meetings:
a practical guide.
1. Corporate meetings—Law and legislation—England 2. Corporate meetings—England
I. Title
658.4′563′0942 KD2079

ISBN 0-902197-45-2

Library of Congress Cataloging in Publication Data
Roberts, Dennis, 1916–
The administration of company meetings.
Includes index.
1. Corporate meetings. 2. Stockholders' meetings.
I. Title
HD2743.R63 1986 658.4′563 86–10353
ISBN 0-902197-45-2

Designed by Ron Jones

Typeset by Hands Fotoset, Leicester

Printed in Great Britain by St Edmundsbury Press, Bury St Edmunds, Suffolk

Contents

Preface

This is not just another book on the law of meetings. Rather it is a practical guide on how to run successful company meetings – and how to run them better.

It should therefore prove useful to every company secretary and every company chairman for guidance on the sound practical administration of company meetings (including board meetings), but it will appeal particularly to the secretary or chairman of the medium or larger company, where meetings are more than a formality, where good presentation is important for public relations, but where something unexpected could call for urgent guidance from a reliable and comprehensive work of reference. The student, too, will find it useful to supplement other textbooks, which all too often emphasise legal background rather than the practical requirements which are the purpose of this volume.

During more than 30 years as secretary and/or director of many companies, public and private, I have attended (and in many cases have handled the administration for) hundreds of board meetings and many annual general meetings. Most ran smoothly, some were brief and formal, but one or two proved turbulent and acrimonious, when survival depended on competence and impartiality.

All this experience I have tried to encapsulate in the present volume for the benefit of those who may still have such problems and opportunities before them.

July 1986 Dennis Roberts

CHAPTER 1

The company meeting: its purpose and importance

What is the purpose of a company meeting?

The purist would answer that the purpose of any meeting is to conduct business, i.e. to make business decisions. Anything not contributing to that end, he would argue, has no place in a business meeting. So meetings should comprise a series of formal questions to be discussed, decided and recorded. Anything else is not strictly relevant to the business of a meeting and should be avoided. However, this view is rather outdated.

Small companies often reach business decisions without a meeting. If the business is of sufficient importance to need a formal record, a 'resolution in writing' will be signed by all those entitled to vote, a practice specifically authorised by articles of association. Even very large companies reach decisions on matters of importance by proxy votes cast on a poll – in effect, a postal ballot – and this is a far more democratic procedure than a show of hands at a poorly attended meeting.

It can be argued that no shareholder should vote until he has attended the meeting and heard what others have to say. There is some force in this, but those best able to guide others may be least able to spare time to attend meetings and have least debating skill. A well-drafted circular, despatched by post and carefully considered at leisure, may be a more reliable guide for the undecided than a vigorous display of forensic art.

Many would argue that the real purpose of a company meeting today is public relations. Everything else can be handled without a meeting, but a company will be judged by the press, by the public and by its shareholders on the way its annual general meeting is conducted. An orderly meeting, well planned and well conducted, will show that the chairman, the directors, the secretary and other senior management know their business and can influence decisions. Not only will they influence the subject under discussion; they will ensure shareholder support for some future, more urgent or more contentious occasion. That should, at the very least, be worth a few extra pence on the price of a public listed company.

Conversely, the annual general meeting is the time when the directors have to answer for their stewardship. Some may bask in the glory of a satisfactory year's progress, but others (perhaps all, sooner or later) must face the shareholders to explain why profits are not up to expectations, why opportunities have been missed. The author remembers one senior business manager, a man of undoubted ability, a skilled negotiator who could secure an order when all seemed lost, who would deal firmly but tactfully with staff and unions, but who admitted his great fear, his major motivation, was the thought of having to answer to the shareholders at the end of the year.

For all these reasons the company meeting deserves careful preparation in every aspect – and for the benefit of every participant. That is the objective of this book.

CHAPTER 2

Law of company meetings

The company secretary or chairman need not be a lawyer, but he needs to know where to find the answers to legal problems as they arise. Often there will be no time to consult legal advisers during the urgent pressures of a meeting, and so he will turn to the Companies Act without finding what he is seeking. Often he would do better to turn to the company's own articles of association, but even the Act and the articles together will not provide a complete guide to the law.

Where, then, is the law of company meetings to be found?

Sources of the law on meetings

The Companies Act 1985

The Companies Act 1985 is of course paramount. We shall refer to it throughout this book as 'the Act'. Only a small part of the Act is concerned with meetings, mainly sections 366 to 383, and these are reproduced in Appendix B to this book. The Act deals only with certain major points; most details relating to meetings are governed not by the Act but by each company's articles of association. Indeed, section 370 of the Act applies only if there are no contrary provisions in the articles, and so, while on most matters the Act is paramount, section 370 can be overruled by the articles.

Companies are also subject to other legislation, such as the Interpretation Act 1978. This governs the interpretation of every subsequent Act of Parliament and statutory instrument. Thus it interprets not only the Act itself but also Table A, which forms part of a statutory instrument, and hence also a company's own articles where these rely on Table A.

The Interpretation Act provides, *inter alia*, that masculine terms include the feminine and vice versa and that references to the singular include the plural and vice versa. Thus 'chairman' includes a woman occupying that office, the right to appoint a proxy includes the right to appoint more than one, while the limited power of continuing directors includes power for a sole remaining director. There are also definitions of 'person' (which includes a company) and 'writing' (which includes typing, printing, photocopying, etc.), but these are unlikely to cause difficulty.

Articles of association

Articles of association are usually of greater immediate relevance to a specific problem than is the Act itself.

Most companies register their own articles of association to meet their particular requirements. If a company does not register articles, then Table A from the Companies Act under which the company was registered will apply as if Table A were the company's articles. If the company does register articles, it may (and usually will) exclude Table A in whole or in part, but, to the extent that special articles neither exclude nor are inconsistent with it, Table A will apply to that company.

In part, Table A merely reiterates statutory requirements, presumably to present a reasonably complete picture within one document. On other matters Table A (or special articles registered for a particular company) will cover such important points as the manner of giving notice, requirements for a quorum, who shall take the chair and whether he has a casting vote, voting rights and the right to demand a poll. The regulations of The Stock Exchange require additional provisions in the articles of a company whose shares or other securities are 'listed' on it.

Table A from the schedule to the Companies (Tables A to F) Regulations 1985 is reproduced as Appendix A to this book. It is important to remember that this latest version of Table A applies only to companies registered under the Companies Act 1985 or to companies which by express wording of their articles have specifically adopted this version of Table A. For other companies, registered under earlier Acts, the relevant Table A will be that scheduled to the Act under which they were registered.

Common law

On many matters, such as the rules of debate, neither the Act nor Table A nor special articles will give any guidance. On such points, one must have regard to general rules representing custom and practice established over many years for the proper conduct of business meetings – not necessarily or exclusively company meetings. These comprise the common law of meetings. Many such rules have been recognised by the courts and confirmed by legal decisions. On other matters, established practices may never have been brought before the courts, perhaps because they were regarded as too obvious to need testing. They must still be regarded, however, as part of the common law. The absence of a leading case on a particular point proves nothing.

As a last resort, if the Act, articles, Table A and common law are all silent, points of procedure will be under the control of the meeting itself. The chairman may be appointed by the board pursuant to the articles, but it is from the meeting that he derives his powers. Usually articles will empower him to resolve minor points of procedure, and, indeed, he may sometimes need to do so if the meeting is to make progress; but, subject to the articles, he must always carry out the wishes of the majority, especially on such matters as when to close discussion and take a vote, or whether to adjourn the meeting.

Majority rule

A company is owned and ultimately controlled by its members or shareholders who exercise their powers by majority vote in general (shareholders') meeting. To this general rule, however, there are exceptions.

A company may act only within the law and within its own powers as set out in the objects clause of its memorandum of association. Its method of operation may be restricted by agreement or by its own articles of association, but subject to that the will of the majority is paramount.

Under the Companies Act 1985 certain things may be done only by the shareholders in general meeting. In most cases (including, for example, an increase in the authorised share capital) an ordinary resolution passed by a bare majority is sufficient, but in other cases (broadly, any change in the constitution of the company, such as a change of name, of objects or in the articles) a special resolution is necessary, requiring a three-fourths majority.

The majority cannot, however, break the law (for example, they must not commit a fraud) and they cannot act *ultra vires*, outside the powers of the company itself. Section 35 of the Act will protect third parties against *ultra vires* acts by the company, but it will not protect the shareholders from one another.

If by the articles the shareholders have delegated certain powers to the directors, or to a managing director, even a majority of the shareholders cannot vote to overrule those powers. (They may be able to remove the directors and appoint others, or they may be able to alter the articles to withdraw the powers, but that is another question.)

Subject to these exceptions, however, procedure at company meetings is protected by a group of legal decisions conveniently referred to as 'The Rule in *Foss* v. *Harbottle*', a case heard in 1843. In his summing-up in that case the judge said: 'If an act, which might be done with the approval of a majority, be done irregularly and without such authority, then the majority are the only persons who can complain.' This has been followed and extended on several occasions, and in *Browne* v. *La Trinidad* (1887) it was said: 'It is most important that the Court should hold fast to the rule upon which it has always acted, not to interfere for the purpose of forcing companies to conduct their business according to the strictest rules, where the irregularity complained of can be set right at any moment.'

To sum up, the law will always protect the majority, provided it acts within the law and *intra vires* the company's powers, and will protect the minority from a fraud or other wrongful or oppressive acts by the majority, but the courts will not interfere on a mere technical irregularity, even a breach of the Act, if it is a matter of the internal management of the company which could and would be rectified by a majority (in certain cases a three-fourths majority) of the members.

CHAPTER 3

General meetings

A general meeting is a meeting of the shareholders of a company. It may also be called a company meeting, a members' meeting or a shareholders' meeting. All these terms mean 'general meeting' but are sometimes used to emphasise the distinction from a board meeting, which is a meeting of directors.

General meetings must conform to the common law and to the Companies Act 1985 (here referred to as the 'Act'), principally sections 366 to 383, reproduced in Appendix B. General meetings of a particular company must also conform to its articles of association or, if it has not registered articles or if on a particular point it has not excluded Table A, then to Table A of the Companies Act under which it was registered.

The precise requirements of the Act and the articles will depend on the type of meeting.

Requirements for a valid meeting

To be valid, a general meeting must be: (1) convened by proper notice; (2) properly constituted; and (3) conducted in compliance with the Act and the company's articles.

Notice is considered in detail in the next chapter. For the meeting to be properly constituted, it must have the right person in the chair and there must be sufficient members present to constitute a quorum.

Chairman

A meeting cannot be held without a chairman, since he is the person responsible for the actual conduct of the meeting. His appointment is a practical necessity rather than a statutory requirement. There is nothing in the Act to say who shall take the chair. That is left to the company's articles or, if they are silent, to the vote of the meeting.

The company's articles almost invariably provide (as in regulation 91 of Table A) that the directors may appoint one of their number to be chairman of the board and may remove him and appoint another. (It will be seen that he is appointed chairman of the *board*, not chairman of the company.) Sometimes there is provision for the appointment of one or more deputy chairmen.

The articles usually also provide (as in regulation 42 of Table A) that the chairman of the board shall preside as chairman at any general meeting. They usually continue by providing for some other director to preside if the chairman is absent or unwilling to act, or for the members present to elect a chairman if no director is present or no director is willing to act. The chairman's powers are discussed in Chapter 5.

Quorum

A meeting requires at least two persons at the same place at the same time. Anything less is not a meeting. Business decisions may be made by correspondence, by telephone or in other ways, and articles usually provide that written agreement by the requisite number of members shall be as effectual as a meeting, but if a meeting is required then at least two persons must actually meet.

There are exceptions. If there is only one holder of shares of a particular class, that shareholder will constitute a meeting of that class, while the court under section 371 of the Act or the Department of Trade and Industry under section 367 may give directions for the holding of meetings which could include a direction that one person (or one proxy) shall, exceptionally, constitute a meeting.

A quorum is the minimum number required to be present before business can be conducted. The number of persons required for a quorum is not specified in the Act, but provision will invariably be found in the company's articles. For example, regulation 40 of Table A requires that at a general meeting two persons entitled to vote shall be a quorum, while for board meetings regulation 89 provides that the board may fix its own quorum, but until and unless it does so the quorum shall be two.

In counting the quorum, proxies and corporate representatives may be included, but when checking whether two persons are present to constitute a meeting regard must be had to *persons* attending. Thus if there are three shareholders, A, B and C, two being required for a quorum, and A appoints B as his proxy while C appoints D as his proxy, then a quorum could comprise any two of A, B and C or any two of A, B and D. But B (in his own right) plus B (as proxy for A) will not be sufficient since only one person is present. Similarly C and D will not form a quorum since only one shareholder is present or represented.

This example would be equally valid if one or more of the shareholders had appointed a representative under section 375 of the Act instead of a proxy. A wholly owned subsidiary, for example, often has two corporate shareholders. Whether they appoint representatives or proxies, it is important that they appoint different persons; otherwise there can be no meeting.

Subject to the articles, 'persons' for this purpose means persons entitled to attend and vote. The fact that proxies vote only on a poll does not prevent them being counted in the quorum even though no poll may be demanded.

However, persons entitled to attend but not to vote (for example, directors who are present but are not shareholders) cannot be counted towards the quorum.

Older forms of articles sometimes require only that 'a quorum must be present when the meeting proceeds to business'. It has been held that in such a case business can still be transacted although one or more persons have left the meeting so that a quorum is no longer present; but the common-law requirement for at least two persons remains.

Modern articles avoid doubt by providing that 'no business shall be transacted at any meeting unless a quorum is present'. If attendance is reduced below a quorum (and it would be one of the duties of the secretary to watch for this), then the chairman has no option but to close (or adjourn) the meeting.

Special rules apply to class meetings, which are discussed later.

If it is not possible to find a quorum to attend a meeting, application can be made to the court for directions which could include a quorum below that specified by the articles, or even a quorum of one person.

Types of meeting

Annual and extraordinary meetings

General meetings are usually either annual general meetings or extraordinary general meetings. The fundamental difference between these is that every company must hold one (and only one) annual general meeting every year, and must give 21 clear days' notice of that meeting. It can hold as many extraordinary general meetings as it wishes, but need not hold any. The notice for an extraordinary general meeting is 21 clear days if a special resolution is to be considered, otherwise 14 clear days for a limited company or 7 clear days for an unlimited company. (The meaning of 'clear days' is explained in more detail on page 13.)

It is sometimes supposed that the difference between an annual general meeting and an extraordinary general meeting lies in the nature of the business to be conducted, but this is not so. Any business can (subject to adequate length of notice) be conducted at either type of meeting. It is true that annual general meetings usually consider annual business, such as the accounts and matters related to the accounts (dividends, re-election of directors and auditors, auditors' remuneration), while extraordinary general meetings usually consider exceptional items such as special resolutions; but there is no reason why either type of business should not be considered at either type of meeting.

Class meetings

Class meetings are required only where the share capital of the company is divided into different classes and it is proposed to vary the rights attaching to one or more of these classes.

Detailed requirements for such a variation are set out in sections 125 to 129 of the Act and depend upon whether the class rights are prescribed by the memorandum of association or the articles or neither, and whether power to vary the rights is set out in one or other of these documents or neither.

Subject to the articles, a class meeting is similar to an extraordinary general meeting except that only holders of the relevant class of shares are entitled to notice or to attend and vote.

The class meeting will be followed by a general meeting of all classes of members which will consider a special resolution to give effect to the variation of rights. This general meeting will follow the usual rules for general meetings but with one important difference: holders of the separate class of shares (e.g. preference shareholders) may not be entitled to vote at other general meetings, but articles usually give them that right if, as on a variation of rights, their interests are 'directly affected'. This is discussed more fully in Chapter 7, where detailed consideration is also given to the rather strict interpretation of the words 'directly affected'.

When two or more meetings are held in quick succession, it is often difficult to prevent one class of shareholders, say, the ordinary shareholders, attending the separate class meeting for, say, the preference shareholders. Their attendance will not invalidate the proceedings, but care should be taken to count only the votes of those entitled to vote at the particular meeting. It will help the chairman if holders of different classes of shares are asked to sit in separate parts of the room, but this can be complicated if many members hold shares of more than one class. A workable alternative is to send different classes of members attendance cards of different colours which they can raise to vote on a show of hands.

The quorum for a class meeting to vary class rights is prescribed by section 125(6), which overrides any provision in the articles. The quorum is two persons (shareholders or proxies) holding or representing at least one-third in nominal value of the issued shares of the class in question. However, for an adjourned class meeting, section 125(6) prescribes the quorum at only one person (or his proxy) holding shares of that class.

It will be seen that this provides an exception to the common-law rule that one person cannot constitute a meeting – at an adjourned class meeting one person will not only constitute a meeting but constitute a quorum. There is another exception: if all the shares of a class are held by one person, that person will suffice to constitute a class meeting, section 125(6) notwithstanding. However, the written consent of that one shareholder would doubtless be more convenient than a meeting!

If the need for a separate class meeting arises from section 125 rather than from the company's memorandum or articles, then the written consent of the holders of three-quarters by nominal value of that class of share may be substituted for the class meeting. If the need for the meeting arises from the articles, a similar provision may be included.

Section 125(6) also provides that at a class meeting any one holder of shares of that class may demand a poll.

Where shares of a separate class are widely held, it can be very difficult to secure a quorum of one-third of the holders. Every encouragement should of course be given for members to return forms of proxy since these are counted towards the quorum, but, even so, many companies resign themselves to the prospect of an adjournment. Since the general meeting of all the members cannot pass resolutions to bring into effect the scheme as a whole until each separate class meeting has given its sanction, this could mean that adjournment of a class meeting will lead to adjournment of the general meeting.

In practice, this problem can easily be circumvented. The actual alteration to the class rights will almost always require a special resolution and hence 21 clear days' notice. The preliminary consents to be given at the class meetings will usually require only an extraordinary resolution and therefore only 14 clear days' notice. All notices can thus be sent out on the same day with a footnote to the notice of each class meeting, called after 14 clear days, to the effect that if there is no quorum at the meeting it will be adjourned to the same time and place seven days later. If a quorum is forthcoming after 14 days, all is well with seven days in hand. If not, all meetings can be held in quick succession after a total of 21 clear days.

Meetings of debenture holders

These are analogous in many ways to class meetings, but debenture holders are creditors of the company, not members. There are no provisions regulating debenture holders' meetings in the Act, and any meetings are governed not by the articles but by the trust deed securing the debentures. These usually follow rules similar to those governing general meetings of members, but reference should be made to the trust deed to find any special provisions applying to a particular series of debentures.

Meetings to commence winding up

Voluntary winding up is initiated by a resolution of the members in general meeting. It must be distinguished from winding up by the court, which commences with a petition to the court. Section 572 of the Act sets out three circumstances which can give rise to such a resolution.

If the articles provide that the company shall be dissolved on the expiry of a fixed duration or on the occurrence of a specified event, then, when the date arrives or the event occurs, the company in general meeting may resolve that the company be wound up voluntarily. An ordinary resolution is sufficient. It can be passed at an extraordinary general meeting, requiring 14 clear days' notice, but in these rather special circumstances it is usually preferable to present it at an annual general meeting, requiring 21 clear days.

If the company resolves that it cannot continue by reason of its debts, an extraordinary resolution is required, the length of notice again being determined by the type of meeting.

In any other circumstances a special resolution is necessary and that requires 21 days' notice irrespective of the type of meeting.

As explained in the next chapter, members holding 95 per cent of the voting rights at an extraordinary general meeting (or 100 per cent in the case of an annual general meeting) can waive the full period of notice, but, unless the directors are able to make a statutory declaration of solvency under section 577 of the Act, the winding up will become a creditors' voluntary winding up and the minimum period of notice to members becomes seven days under section 588: this period cannot be shortened by waiver.

As winding up progresses, meetings of creditors and of members (now called 'contributories') will be required, but that is a matter of insolvency administration, outside the scope of this book.

Statutory meetings

The requirement for all public companies to hold a 'statutory meeting' between one and three months after becoming entitled to commence business was abolished by the Companies Act 1980.

CHAPTER 4

Notice of the meeting

A valid meeting requires valid notice.

Contents of valid notice

Valid notice must state the date, time and place of the meeting. If it is an annual general meeting, the notice must say so. The business of the meeting must be stated in enough detail to enable the member receiving it to understand the purpose of the meeting sufficiently to decide whether or not to attend. If the business includes a special resolution or an extraordinary resolution, then the exact wording of the resolution must be set out. If the company has share capital, the notice must state that a member entitled to attend is entitled to appoint a proxy (or more than one proxy if that is allowed) and that a proxy need not also be a member.

Draft wording for the notice of an annual general meeting, the business of which includes a special resolution, will be found in Appendix G. This wording can readily be adapted for other types of meeting.

If the company's shares are listed on The Stock Exchange, an explanatory circular must be sent with the notice for all other than routine business, or, where such business is to be conducted at an annual general meeting or at a separate meeting on the same day as the annual general meeting, an explanation must be given in the directors' report.

Length of notice

Length of notice depends on the type of meeting and the business to be conducted, as explained in the previous chapter, but briefly to recapitulate: an annual general meeting or a meeting to consider a special resolution requires 21 clear days' notice. An extraordinary general meeting which does not include a special resolution requires 14 clear days' notice for a limited company or 7 clear days for an unlimited company. However, since extraordinary general meetings are usually called to consider special resolutions for which 21 clear days' notice is required, both types of meeting in practice usually require 21 clear days. The company's articles can extend (but not relax) the requirements of the Act, but this is now unusual.

There is one other case in which 21 days' notice is appropriate for an extraordinary general meeting. Section 241 of the Act requires every company in each financial year to lay copies of its accounts before the company in general meeting. This can be either the annual general meeting or an extraordinary general meeting. However, section 240 of the Act requires that a copy of the accounts be sent 21 days before the meeting to every member of the company and to every debenture holder. It is obviously convenient to send the notice of the meeting with the accounts 21 clear days in advance, irrespective of the type of meeting.

Special notice

To elect or re-elect a director who is over the age of 70, to remove a director or auditor, or to appoint as auditor anyone other than the retiring auditor, a procedure known as 'special notice' is required.

Special notice takes two stages. First, any member entitled to vote should give 28 clear days' notice of his intention to propose the motion at the next meeting. Then the company must give notice to members of the proposed resolution at the same time and in the same manner as it gives notice of the meeting – which may be 14 or 21 clear days, according to the *other* business of the meeting. If this second requirement is not practicable, the company may give notice by newspaper advertisement not less than 21 days before the meeting, or in any other manner permitted by the articles.

There is provision against forestalling. If a meeting is called within 28 days after the member has given his notice to the company, the member's notice is deemed properly given. The effect of this is to nullify the '28 days' requirement; the member's notice will be deemed valid if given at any time, however short, before the company sends out the notice calling the meeting.

The member's notice could be worded: 'I hereby give special notice of my intention to propose the following resolution at the next general meeting of the company . . .' It is best handed in at the registered office or, if that is not practicable, then sent by recorded delivery post. (Registered post is normally not good 'notice' *to* a company.) The notice which has then to be given by the company (part of the notice of the meeting) could be worded: 'Special notice has been received from a member of his intention to propose the following resolution . . .'

Usually the person giving special notice to the company will propose the resolution at the meeting, but this is not essential. If special notice has been properly given, anyone may propose the resolution.

Clear days

The term 'clear days' excludes the day on which the notice is served (or deemed served – see below) and the day on which the meeting is held, but subject to this all days (including Saturdays and Sundays) are counted.

Unless articles provide otherwise, the date on which notice of a meeting is served is the day it is received by the person to whom it is addressed. Notice can be given personally by handing it to the member, but it is usually given by post, and, since there can be no certainty of the date of delivery of even first-class letters, this could lead to uncertainty as to the date of service. Articles usually therefore make specific provision on this point. For example, regulation 115 of Table A provides: 'A notice shall . . . be deemed to be given at the expiration of 48 hours after the envelope containing it was posted.'

Thus, if Table A applies and 21 clear days' notice is required, a notice posted on Day 1 will be deemed served on Day 3. Days 4 to 24 inclusive will be the 21 clear days, and the meeting can be held on Day 25. As a quick check, whether 7, 14 or 21 clear days are required, the first clear day and the earliest date for the meeting will be the same day of the week. Longer notice can of course be given.

Regulation 39 of Table A provides: 'The accidental omission to give notice of a meeting . . . or the non-receipt of notice of a meeting . . . shall not invalidate the proceedings at that meeting.' The words 'accidental omission' would cover a minor clerical error or computer fault, even if more than one member failed to receive notice, but would not cover an error of law, e.g. an error as to who was entitled to be sent notice.

Waiver of full period of notice

A meeting can be held at shorter notice than the full statutory period provided sufficient members agree. This may not be much use in the case of a p.l.c. with thousands of members, but can be very useful with a small private company, all of whose members can readily be asked to sign a waiver of the full statutory period.

To waive the full period of notice in the case of an annual general meeting, every member entitled to attend and vote must agree. For any other meeting, a majority holding 95 per cent in nominal value of the shares giving the right to attend and vote is sufficient, or, in the case of a guarantee company not having share capital, members representing not less than 95 per cent of the total voting rights.

Notice must still be given to every member; it is only the full *length* of notice that can be waived. The usual practice is to give every member (or members having at least 95 per cent of the votes) notice in duplicate, the second copy having appended a form of waiver for the member to sign and return.

While it is convenient to have the waiver signed at the foot of the notice, it is not essential. Provided the wording identifies the particular meeting, the waiver could be on a separate sheet or a series of separate sheets. Indeed, a waiver can be given orally. With some very small companies, the chairman will call the shareholders together, hand each a copy of the notice and ask if they agree to the meeting being held forthwith. In whatever way a waiver is arranged, it should be recorded in the minutes of the meeting.

A suitable wording for a form of waiver to be appended to the notice of a meeting might read:

'We, being (all the) members [*or* members holding not less than 95 per cent of the issued share capital] of .... Limited, hereby agree to the meeting being held according to the foregoing notice notwithstanding that less than the full statutory period of notice has been given.'

Who may call a meeting?

The meeting must be called by the board of directors. The company secretary will of course make all the arrangements, including sending out the notice, which he will sign 'by order of the board', but he should do so only on the authority of the board and should include in the agenda only such business as the board has authorised.

There is one exception to this. If members of the company exercise their right to requisition an extraordinary general meeting or to requisition a resolution for the annual general meeting as explained later in this chapter, the company secretary should still, if possible, obtain the authority of a board meeting; but if this is not forthcoming he would be justified in calling the meeting or adding the item to the agenda in accordance with the wishes of the requisitionists, provided of course he is satisfied that the requisitionists have met all the statutory requirements.

Articles usually include a provision on the lines of regulation 90 of Table A to the effect that, if the number of directors is reduced below the number fixed as the quorum, then the continuing director or directors may act, but only for the purpose of filling the vacancies or of calling a general meeting.

As a last resort, if it is impracticable to call a meeting in any other way, any director or any member of the company entitled to vote may apply to the court under section 371 of the Act to order a meeting to be held. The court may decide how the meeting is to be called, where and when it is to be held and how it is to be conducted. This power is rarely used but provides a means of overcoming any deadlock, e.g. in consequence of unusual provisions in the articles or a series of sudden deaths.

The business of the meeting

Only the board of directors can decide what business is to be included on the agenda for the meeting. They will usually do this at the board meeting at which they resolve to call the meeting, but they can delegate to the secretary, the chairman or anyone else. A sufficient number of members may also requisition a resolution for the agenda as explained later. The point to be stressed, however, is that neither the chairman nor the secretary should include business otherwise than on the authority of the board or pursuant to a valid requisition.

If a meeting is called or business is included without proper authority, the board can ratify the action later. Even the most prudent company secretary may find he needs to 'jump the gun' in an emergency, but he should take care to seek ratification by a board minute at the earliest opportunity. The problem that could arise is that, if proper authority has not been given and until the action has been ratified, a dissident member might apply to the court for an injunction to prohibit the meeting from being held or to prevent the additional business from being discussed.

To whom must notice be given?

Unless there are special provisions in the articles, notice of the meeting must be sent to every member and every member is entitled to attend and vote. Notice (of all meetings, not just the meeting which receives the accounts) must also be sent to the auditors, who are entitled to attend under section 387 of the Act.

Special articles frequently restrict the right to vote (e.g. in the case of preference or non-voting ordinary shares) and sometimes provide that notice need not be sent to members who have no right to vote. However, all members are entitled to copies of the accounts, irrespective of the right to vote.

The personal representatives of deceased members are not members, are not usually entitled to vote, and therefore are not entitled to receive notice, unless they have completed a form of request by which they elect to have the shares registered in their own names. However, while practice varies, it is usually thought better to send notices to personal representatives irrespective of their strict entitlement.

Articles often provide (as in regulation 112 of Table A) that a member not resident in the United Kingdom may give the company an address within the UK to which notices may be sent, but if he has not given such an address then he is not entitled to notice. Note, however, that although a member resident abroad may not be entitled to receive notice he is still entitled to appoint a proxy, while if he arrives at the meeting he is still entitled to admission and to vote.

Where shares are held jointly, the articles usually provide (as in regulation 112 of Table A) that notices shall be given to the first-named holder only. If joint holders wish that they shall both (or all) receive copies, they can split their shareholding into two or more accounts, each account having a different person named first. Although only the first named is entitled to notice, all are entitled to attend the meeting.

Actual notice of the meeting must be given to members and to the auditors even though the members (or 95 per cent of them) may have given a waiver of the full *period* of notice. Moreover, any waiver must be signed by the requisite number of members *entitled to attend and vote*, whether or not they are entitled to notice. Thus members who have not given an address in the United Kingdom for notices must be included when counting the signatures required for a valid waiver. On the other hand, preference shareholders may not be entitled to attend and vote at a particular meeting, in which case they do not need to be taken into account.

If the company's shares are listed on The Stock Exchange, six copies of all notices, circulars, reports and announcements must be sent to The Stock Exchange at the same time as they are issued to members.

All this may be confusing. It has therefore been summarised in the table in Appendix C. It may be useful to photocopy the table, alter A, B and C according to the particular company's articles, and hold copies for quick reference at the door and on the platform.

Accounts: to whom must they be sent?

Any member who is entitled to notice will also be entitled to a copy of the accounts. Moreover, a member may be entitled to the accounts even though he is not entitled to notice. The accounts to be sent comprise the profit and loss account, balance sheet, directors' report and auditors' report, and, where the company has subsidiaries, the group accounts.

Regardless of any restrictions in the articles, section 240 of the Act requires copies of the accounts to be sent: (1) to everyone entitled to notice of general meetings; and (2), if the company has share capital, to every shareholder and to every debenture holder whether or not he is entitled to notice of general meetings. Thus copies of the accounts must be sent to preference shareholders and debenture holders who are not entitled to notice of meetings and also to the auditors because they are entitled to notice of general meetings under section 387 of the Act.

It must be remembered that mortgagees and other secured creditors of the company are, technically, debenture holders and therefore entitled to copies of the accounts. However, the position of holders of unsecured loan stock is far from clear. Such loan stock was once known as 'naked debentures', but the general view today seems to be that unsecured loan stock holders are not debenture holders and not therefore entitled to copies of the accounts.

In the case of joint holders, whether or not entitled to notice, one copy of the accounts is sufficient and this is usually sent to the first named.

Copies of the accounts need not be sent, however, to members or debenture holders (1) who are not entitled to notice *and* (2) of whose addresses the company is unaware.

Oddly, the company is not excused from sending copies of the accounts to persons entitled to notice but of whose addresses the company is unaware! Some companies, in consequence, post off several hundred copies of the accounts every year to, for example, 'John Smith, Esq., Address unknown' and then carefully file the envelopes as returned by the Post Office as evidence that they have complied with the law. This seems pointless. It is doubtful whether the company can be said to have 'sent' copies of the accounts when they know they cannot be delivered, and in any event a prosecution for an inevitable and rather technical breach of the Act seems unthinkable.

Requisitioning a meeting

Members holding one-tenth of the voting rights may requisition an extraordinary general meeting under section 368 of the Act. The procedure is for the requisitionists to sign and deposit at the registered office a requisition requiring the directors to call the meeting and stating the object of the meeting. All may sign on one sheet of paper or they may sign on separate sheets identically worded.

The directors must then convene a meeting within 21 days. If they do not do so, the requisitionists may themselves convene the meeting, acting as nearly as possible as the directors would act in convening a meeting. Either way, the meeting must be held within three months from the date the requisition was deposited.

If the directors convene the meeting, the cost will fall on the company, but, if the directors default and the requisitionists convene the meeting, the cost will initially fall on the requisitionists. However, section 368(6) requires the company to reimburse the requisitionists' reasonable expenses and requires the company also to recover the cost by retaining the money out of fees and other remuneration due to the defaulting directors.

Requisitioning a resolution

Instead of requisitioning a meeting, dissident shareholders may requisition a resolution to be included in the agenda for the next annual general meeting. As a further alternative they may provide the directors with a statement not exceeding 1,000 words in respect of any business to be dealt with at the annual general meeting and require them to circulate it to all members entitled to receive notice of the meeting.

The advantage is that these procedures require the support of only 5 per cent – or less – of the voting rights, compared with 10 per cent to requisition a meeting. The disadvantage is that, while the cost of a requisitioned meeting falls on the company (or on the directors), the cost of circulating an additional resolution or a statement could fall on the requisitionists. However, the cost of a circular should not be heavy and it may be possible to pass the cost back to the company as explained below.

The procedure is for one or more members holding at least 5 per cent of the voting rights, or 100 or more members holding shares on which an average £100 has been paid up, to sign and deposit at the registered office of the company a requisition under section 376 of the Act enclosing the statement to be circulated or setting out the wording of the resolution to be included on the agenda, with payment sufficient to cover the cost of circulation. If a resolution is requisitioned, it must be deposited at least six weeks before the annual general meeting; if a statement, then one week before is sufficient. There is provision against forestalling by the directors – if an otherwise valid requisition is deposited and the annual general meeting is then called within six weeks, the requisition will be deemed to have been deposited in time. All can sign on one piece of paper or signatures can be on any number of separate forms, each identically worded.

While the cost falls initially on the requisitionists, they must be reimbursed if the company so decides. The usual practice, therefore, is to include in the requisition a resolution requiring reimbursement of expenses.

The directors must then give notice of the resolution and/or send out copies of the statement, if possible at the same time as the notice of the meeting, or if this is not possible then as soon as practicable thereafter.

As a safeguard against misuse of this procedure, any person aggrieved may apply to the court to prevent the circulation of the statement on the grounds that the statutory provision is being used to secure needless publicity for defamatory matter.

CHAPTER 5

The business of the meeting: resolutions

The business of a meeting is to reach decisions. Accordingly the meeting is conducted as a series of proposals which may be termed 'propositions' or 'motions' or (perhaps incorrectly) 'resolutions'.

It would be out of order for anyone (other than the chairman) to speak at the meeting unless a proposition was before it. It would be equally out of order for anyone to speak other than about the proposition currently under discussion. Each proposition is discussed in its turn and voted upon. Only when a decision has been reached (or, for good reason and after following the proper procedure, a decision has been deferred) can the meeting turn to the next business.

This may seem elementary, but it is worth stating – indeed, emphasising – because failure to observe these elementary rules of procedure can lead to problems and confusion.

To all rules there are exceptions. The chairman may need to speak other than to the proposition under discussion, e.g. to call the meeting to order. Any person entitled to speak may raise a point of order, i.e. a formal point relating to the conduct of the meeting rather than the business under discussion. Some items of business do not lend themselves readily to the basic formula of always having a proposition before the meeting, although such exceptions should be rare.

For example, if the chairman opens the meeting by asking the secretary to read the notice convening it, there is at that point no proposition before the meeting, and so some chairmen bring the proceedings within the rules by formally proposing that the notice be taken as read – and even asking shareholders to vote upon it. In fact this is quite unnecessary and happily it is now rare. It is not necessary to read the notice at all. It is now more usual to save time by starting straight into the business on the basis that members would not be there if they had not read the notice. Similarly, if one of the shareholders wishes to thank the chairman and/or the board of directors, this will be presented as a proposal, a vote of thanks.

Difficulties can arise over the auditors' report, which must be 'read before the company in general meeting' (section 241(2) of the Act), but even here the custom is often to propose the adoption of the accounts and then to read the auditors' report as an introduction to discussion of the proposal to adopt the accounts.

Each proposition must be proposed. It is usually seconded, but this is not essential. It may be discussed and questions may be addressed to the chairman as part of that discussion. It may be amended. On a controversial subject the proposer may exercise a right of reply. At the conclusion of discussion the chairman must call for a vote by show of hands, after which a poll may be demanded, in which event the chairman will decide whether the poll is to be taken there and then or at some other time. The meeting then proceeds to the next item of business.

The question of voting, including polls and proxies, justifies a chapter to itself (Chapter 6), but the other points of procedure will be considered in detail here.

Resolutions generally

Strictly speaking, a resolution is something that has been resolved; a proposition is not a resolution until it has been put to the meeting and resolved, i.e. carried by an affirmative vote. Thus it is still often the practice to refer to a proposal up to the time that it is voted upon as a 'motion' or a 'proposition'. This is certainly desirable if there is any danger of uncertainty as to whether the matter has or has not been decided. But in circumstances where no dubiety can arise there is a growing practice of using the word 'resolution' (or even 'proposed resolution') throughout, as in section 376 of the Act, or regulation 46 of Table A.

A motion or resolution, when before the meeting, is sometimes termed 'the question'.

Care must be taken with the wording of resolutions. The wording proposed will become the decision of the meeting and the wording for the minutes. Any ambiguity should be eliminated before the matter is voted upon.

It is therefore preferable that all propositions and amendments, other than purely procedural motions, should be put in writing at the earliest opportunity. The wording of a resolution arising from an item on the agenda will appear in the chairman's extended agenda and should also be made available to the person intending to propose it, either as a copy of the extended agenda or typed separately. (It could conveniently be typed on a small card.) If the proposition arises from the floor of the meeting, the proposer should be asked to put it in writing – and provided with pen and paper for this purpose.

The same procedure can be adopted for amendments, but if practicable it is usually better to provide the mover of the amendment with a copy of the original proposition on which he can show the alterations he wishes to make. Often the proposer will be adept at wording his proposal, but when necessary the secretary should be ready to assist.

The wording of resolutions requires skill and practice, and the examples given in Appendices J, L and M may help. It may also help to set out some general principles:

1. Every resolution should commence with 'that'. One reason is to avoid the necessity to vary the wording as the matter proceeds: the proposer can say

'I propose that . . .', the chairman can announce 'It has been proposed that . . .', or 'I now ask you to vote on the proposal that . . .', while the minutes can be worded 'It was resolved that . . .'. Without this elementary standardisation the secretary may find he cannot draft minutes grammatically without altering the wording of the resolution.

2. If possible, the whole resolution should be included in a single sentence. If this would be too cumbersome, the second sentence should also commence 'that . . .' or (preferably) 'It is (was) further resolved that . . .'.
3. As far as possible, resolutions should be affirmative rather than negative.
4. Precision is essential, especially where dates or sums of money are concerned. For example, a resolution 'that Mr X be appointed a director' leaves some doubt as to when he takes office. It would be better to resolve 'that Mr X be *and is hereby* appointed a director', or 'that Mr X be appointed a director *to take office on and after 1st January next*'. Particular care is needed with dividend resolutions, which should state as a minimum: (1) the dividend per share; (2) the payment date; and (3) the record date.
5. The word 'should' often leads to ambiguity and is better avoided. Consider: 'It was resolved that Mr X *should* be appointed a director.' Has the meeting appointed him or do they merely think it a good idea, to be considered further at a later date? It is usually sufficient simply to delete the word 'should'.
6. The proposed resolution must be in such form that it can be answered with a simple 'yes' or 'no'. Three-way voting is just not practicable and can lead to uncertainty as to what the meeting really wanted.
7. The resolution must be within the powers of the company, as expressed in its memorandum and articles, and also within the powers of the meeting. The presumption of legality given by section 35 of the Act runs only in favour of third parties, not other shareholders. Moreover, a resolution will be *ultra vires* (regardless of the memorandum and articles) if it is illegal or contrary to public policy.
8. The resolution must be within the scope of the meeting; i.e. it must be covered by the notice. (See also Chapter 4.)

Ordinary, special and extraordinary resolutions

An ordinary resolution is any resolution other than a special resolution or an extraordinary resolution. An ordinary resolution may be passed by a simple majority. It is sufficient for any business unless a special or extraordinary resolution is required by the Act or by the company's articles.

In certain circumstances, as explained in Chapter 4, special *notice* is required of an ordinary resolution. This must not be confused with a special *resolution*.

A special resolution is required by the Act for any change in the constitution of the company other than an increase in capital. Thus a special resolution is required for a change in the name, the objects clause or the articles, or for a resolution that the company be wound up voluntarily.

3. The mover of an amendment does not (unless articles so provide) have a right of reply. The proposer of the original motion retains his right of reply, but he must of course speak to the substantive motion. If he feels the amendments are so substantial that they have frustrated his original intention, he is quite entitled to use his right of reply to speak against the motion he originally proposed.
4. An amendment must be moved during the discussion on the original (or the substantive, amended) proposition. It cannot be moved after the original question has been put to the vote.

Usually amendments are proposed, discussed and voted upon one at a time. Sometimes a second amendment is proposed before the first is disposed of, in which case the amendments are usually discussed in the order in which they are proposed. Occasionally it may be necessary to ask the proposer of the first amendment if he will agree to the meeting discussing the amendments in logical order, i.e. the order in which they affect the wording of the original motion.

Sometimes an amendment is proposed to an amendment. This can confuse the meeting, the members and, not least, the chairman. Handling such a situation can call for considerable tact.

Some chairmen refuse sub-amendments, but it is doubtful whether they are entitled to do so. If a sub-amendment is accepted, there can be doubt whether the sub-amendment should be discussed first or whether the main amendment should be discussed first so that the sub-amendment becomes an amendment to the substantive motion. The latter course is preferable, but the legal position is far from clear.

Probably the best course is to steer members away from making amendments to amendments by suggesting an alternative wording which would operate as a direct amendment to the substantive motion. For example, the main amendment may propose insertion of the words 'with effect from 1st January 1986'. A member who proposes deletion of '1st January' and substitution of '15th February' could be asked to wait until the main amendment – the general idea of inserting a date – has been voted upon. If the main amendment is carried, he can then propose his original amendment as an amendment to the substantive motion; if the main amendment is lost, he can still propose insertion of the words 'with effect from 15th February 1986'. The final result will be the same, but it avoids confusing the meeting.

Voting

When all members have had an opportunity to speak (or a fair cross-section, as explained above), the chairman should bring the discussion to a close and call upon the members to vote. Voting, with the related questions of proxies and polls, is covered in Chapter 6, but it should be mentioned here that voting must first be by show of hands. Only when the chairman has announced the motion carried or lost (adding, if he wishes to emphasise the point, 'on a show of hands') can a poll be demanded. The chairman must then announce whether the poll will be taken there and then or at some other time. If a poll is not demanded, or when the chairman has announced when and where it will be held, the meeting will proceed to the next business on the agenda.

Points of order

Points of order (not to be confused with procedural motions) are matters relating to the conduct or regularity (or more often the irregularity!) of the proceedings to which the speaker wishes to draw the chairman's attention. For example, a member may wish to draw attention to the fact that a motion is not covered by the notice of the meeting, or that a quorum is no longer present, or that the tellers have not counted all the votes on a show of hands. A point of order may be raised at any time during the meeting, even by a member who has already spoken on the subject then under discussion.

Explanations should be factual and brief. No discussion is permitted. The chairman must rule immediately whether any irregularity has occurred, and, if so, how he proposes to rectify it. After rectification (if that is possible) the business of the meeting is resumed.

Procedural motions

Procedural motions also relate to the conduct of the meeting but refer not to any irregularity but to a proposal to change the course of the meeting. There are six main procedural motions, as follows:

1. *Closure*

'That the question be now put.'

The purpose of the closure motion is to bring discussion to an end and reach a decision. It is not discussed. As soon as the closure has been moved and seconded, the chairman must ask the meeting to vote on the closure. If it is carried, discussion is closed and the substantive motion is also put to the vote without further discussion. The meeting then proceeds to the next business. If the closure motion is lost, discussion on the substantive motion continues. The chairman has no discretion to refuse the closure motion, except that, if it is moved a second time shortly after an earlier attempt has failed, he can defer the closure vote for a short while.

2. *Previous question*

'That the question be *not* now put.'

Students often find the term 'previous question' puzzling, but it must be remembered that 'previous' can mean 'premature'.

The objective of the previous question is to end the discussion without reaching a decision. This could frustrate the purpose of the meeting and the motion should therefore not be treated lightly. Accordingly (unlike the closure motion), it can be debated. If it is carried, the meeting will proceed to the next business without voting on the substantive motion, or if there is no further business the meeting will end. If the previous question is lost, discussion on the substantive motion resumes.

3. *To proceed to the next business*

This is self-explanatory. The effect is similar to that of the previous question motion, except that the motion is voted upon immediately, without discussion. It can be moved only if there is other business to discuss, and, when all other business is completed, the meeting returns to the unfinished business.

4. *To adjourn*

This is a motion to suspend discussion now with a view to resuming it later. It may be a motion (1) to adjourn the meeting or (2) to adjourn the discussion on that item of business.

On a motion to adjourn the meeting, the proposer may indicate the date, time and place at which he proposes the meeting should resume, or he may leave it to the chairman to make some suggestion after discussion with his board colleagues. A frequent arrangement is the same day and time in the following week and at the same place, but it would be prudent to check that the room will be available! Articles often provide that fresh notice is not required if adjournment is for a period not exceeding seven days, but in this event it would of course be essential to announce, before the meeting breaks up, the date, time and place at which it will be resumed.

A motion to adjourn the debate may specify no time for resumption, in which event the discussion will be adjourned to appear on the agenda for the next meeting. Alternatively, and not infrequently, it will specify that discussion of that item of business is to be resumed at the end of the meeting after all other business has been completed. This is a convenient way of ensuring that routine business is not squeezed out at the end of the meeting by an early debate that has provoked more discussion than expected.

5. *That the proposer be permitted to withdraw the motion*

Sometimes a proposal meets unexpected opposition and the proposer wishes he had never raised the subject, but neither he nor the chairman can end it unless the meeting agrees. However, if the proposer says he wishes to withdraw, the chairman should ask the meeting to vote on the formal motion that the proposer be permitted to withdraw the proposition. If the motion is carried, the meeting proceeds to the next business.

A motion can, of course, only be withdrawn if in fact it has been proposed. Occasionally, even after special notice, no one can be found to propose a motion. The meeting then proceeds to the next business without further formality.

6. *Reference back*

This can arise only when the meeting is discussing a recommendation from some other body, such as the board of directors or a committee. The motion usually requests that the report under discussion, or some aspect of it, be referred back to the committee for further consideration and revision. The motion may also indicate the date by which the meeting wishes to receive a revised report.

At parliamentary and local government meetings the motion to refer back is sometimes used to express strong disagreement with the recommendations in the report, but at company and other business meetings it usually indicates that discussion has uncovered points that do not appear to have been dealt with by the reporting committee, which should therefore be given the opportunity for further consideration.

CHAPTER 6

Voting, proxies and polls

Shareholders may vote either by a show of hands or on a poll.

A vote must always be taken first by a show of hands. Only when the chairman has declared the result may a poll be demanded. Polls (and proxies) will be considered in detail later, but it will be convenient to consider first the principal features – and differences – between the two methods of voting.

A vote by show of hands is always taken immediately. Every shareholder present in person (including every representative appointed by a corporate member) may cast one vote by raising a hand. Proxies may not vote on a show of hands. Directors who are not shareholders may not vote at a general meeting in any event. When votes (i.e. raised hands) have been counted for and against, the chairman must declare the resolution lost or carried.

Clearly this is an unsatisfactory way of voting. Very few members usually attend a company general meeting and the voting on a show of hands reflects neither the views of those unable to attend nor the fact that some shareholders may have a far greater stake in the company than others. Nevertheless, voting on a show of hands is an essential preliminary to the demand for a poll.

On a poll votes are cast by completing voting papers and they are counted according to size of shareholding. Votes may be cast in person or by proxy. Articles usually provide that on a poll each member shall have one vote for each share (or each £1 stock) he holds, but occasionally members of a particular class may have, say, one vote for every ten shares (or £10 stock) held.

While a show of hands must be taken and the result declared immediately, voting by poll may be taken either immediately or at some other, more convenient, time, e.g. at the end of the meeting or on a later day. Often – indeed, usually – this facility enables votes to be cast in what is effectively a postal ballot.

In practice the outcome of the voting is often a foregone conclusion, but this does not excuse the chairman from asking the members to vote. If all are in favour on a show of hands, or if at least there is no significant opposition, the chairman can declare the result and proceed to the next business; but if there is opposition it will always be prudent to call for a poll. A poll must be properly demanded in accordance with the articles, but the chairman usually has an unassailable right to demand a poll and in many circumstances (e.g. if he knows that a significant number of proxies are against the proposal) it may be his duty as chairman of the meeting, irrespective of his personal inclinations, to use this power to ensure that the ultimate decision reflects the wishes of the members. The decision on a poll is normally above criticism and beyond challenge.

Counting the votes on a show of hands

Clearly it is important, on any contentious issue, to ensure that only valid votes are counted. The next chapter considers in detail who is entitled to vote, and with a small private company where every shareholder is known personally to the chairman no further problems will arise. But at the general meeting of a large public company there will be persons entitled to attend who are not entitled to vote and others who may have not legal entitlement to attend but whom it would be tactless to exclude. After a long and possibly acrimonious discussion it would be all too easy for such people to raise their hands and be counted in error as valid votes.

One way of dealing with this problem is to attempt to segregate voters from non-voters in the arrangement of seating within the room. This is easy with the press, who always appreciate seats at a table on which they can rest their notebooks, but others may prefer to choose their own seats. Only if the agenda includes business which is both important and contentious (and some would argue not even then) could the company be justified in excluding those non-voters who have no right to attend, or in imposing any form of compulsion in regard to seating.

A better course is to provide voting cards, one card of a distinctive colour being issued to each member entitled to vote on a show of hands, either by post with the notice of the meeting or as he enters the door. The latter course is preferred as it reduces the risk of impersonation. Voting cards sent by post may only increase the difficulty of persuading a wife that she is not entitled to vote for her husband, or vice versa!

Occasionally the count on a show of hands is challenged, e.g. on the grounds that the voters in part of the room have not been counted, or that persons not entitled to vote have in fact done so, or that there was misunderstanding as to the exact wording of the proposition. If there is any doubt, and provided the vote is challenged without delay, members should be asked to vote again. It may be appropriate for the chairman first to reread the motion, to restate who is entitled to vote, or to adjudicate on difficult cases.

While the chairman's original declaration of the result will be prima-facie evidence of the result (and once entered in the minute book and signed by the chairman will usually be beyond challenge), a correction made at the earliest practicable opportunity will nullify and supersede the earlier declaration.

As a last resort it can be reassuring to remember that the outcome of voting on a show of hands does not really matter. If the voting is close, if the validity of some votes is suspect, or if there is a suspicion that the result does not really reflect the wishes of the generality of members, then the chairman can demand a poll. On a poll more time and more care can be taken to check the validity of each vote cast.

Casting vote

An ordinary resolution requires a simple majority vote, i.e. *more than* half. If votes for and against are equal, the motion is lost.

However, articles frequently provide (as in regulation 50 of Table A) that on an equality of votes the chairman shall have a casting vote. There is no common-law or statutory right to a casting vote: it depends upon the articles. Indeed, there appears to be a growing practice of omitting from the articles any reference to a casting vote, possibly on the grounds that it looks undemocratic.

The purpose of a casting vote is to serve as a 'tie-breaker'. As we have seen, on an equality of votes the motion is lost, but the inexperienced or the argumentative may be disposed to question this. Use of the casting vote can put the matter beyond doubt.

For this reason it is often suggested that the chairman should always use his casting vote against the motion, to confirm the decision the meeting has already taken. This argument is sound in the majority of cases, but the discretion is the chairman's and his alone and there can be occasions when the casting vote can be better used to ensure the progress of the meeting. In all cases care must obviously be taken to avoid stirring up the controversy the casting vote is intended to resolve.

A better argument may be that the chairman should use his own vote first in his own personal interest (assuming, of course, that he is a shareholder and therefore entitled to vote) and in the event of equality of voting he should then use his casting vote in the interests of the meeting. Seen in this light, there is nothing illogical or inconsistent in using his own vote one way and the casting vote the other; indeed, it can be the mark of a good chairman that he recognises that his duty to the meeting must on occasion override his personal preference.

This said, a good chairman will recognise that the use of the casting vote can be controversial. It may be better to demand a poll.

Note that a casting vote can be used only on an equality of votes. It cannot be used, if voting is close, to create an equality and thus defeat the motion. Equally, no purpose is served by using it on a special or extraordinary resolution. Such a resolution is clearly carried by a 75/25 vote and is equally clearly lost on a 50/50 vote – even if the casting vote would make it 51/50!

Articles of association are usually worded so that the casting vote may also be used on a poll, but, having regard to the far greater number of votes cast on a poll, an equality of votes must be highly improbable.

Proxies

A proxy is a person appointed to vote for another. The appointment must be in writing and the standard, usually printed, form used for this purpose is also often referred to as a 'proxy'. While incorrect, this usage is unobjectionable provided no ambiguity results.

When giving notice of the meeting, the company must, under section 372(3) of the Act, include 'with reasonable prominence a statement that a member entitled to attend and vote is entitled to appoint a proxy'. This usually takes the form of a footnote, printed in type as prominent as that used for the notice itself.

It is common practice, and required under Stock Exchange regulations, to send members forms of proxy which they are invited to complete, appointing as their proxy some person of their choice, or, failing that, the chairman of the meeting.

A variation on this, also required under Stock Exchange regulations, is to provide the member with an opportunity of indicating, in respect of each resolution, how the proxy is to vote. The form is invariably worded so that the member may give no indication, leaving the proxy to vote at his discretion. In practice the use of such forms amounts to a postal ballot of all members, whether or not able to attend the meeting. Proxies given in this form in favour of the chairman of the meeting place on him the duty to use them, irrespective of his own wishes or those of the board, in any case where their use would influence the decision.

A form of proxy covering all these points and meeting Stock Exchange requirements will be found in Appendix K.

Forms of proxy may be sent to shareholders at the company's expense, provided, if they invite the appointment of one person or one of a number of persons (e.g. the chairman of the meeting or any one of the directors), that the forms are sent to all shareholders and not to a selected list. A form of proxy may, however, be sent in response to a specific request.

It can be argued that a poll supported by proxies is the highest form of decision-taking. It offers: (1) a postal ballot; (2) a separate vote on each point at issue; (3) at least two, or more often three, weeks for consideration; (4) an opportunity to leave a blank so that the proxy may listen to the arguments at the meeting before reaching his decision; (5) an opportunity to reverse a decision on a change of heart, either by submitting a second proxy or by turning up in person; and (6) votes counted according to each voter's financial stake.

However, it suffers from one defect: it is not a *secret* ballot. Indeed, since – at least on a controversial issue – all votes must be checked against the register of members, it is difficult to devise procedures that would make it completely secret. However, the nature of company registration work is such that the staff employed must be trustworthy and the chief registrar will be – or certainly should be – a person subject to a professional disciplinary code. Moreover, most companies instruct that after a suitable interval (say, three weeks after the decision is taken) all proxy forms must be destroyed.

Office procedure on receipt of proxies

Articles (as in regulation 62 of Table A) usually require forms of proxy to be completed and returned to the company 48 hours before the meeting or adjourned meeting, or such shorter time as the directors may allow. Table A also permits proxy forms to be returned 24 hours before a poll. Any longer time than 48 hours before a meeting, an adjourned meeting or a poll is proscribed by section 372(5) of the Act.

There is no requirement in the Act that forms of proxy shall be sent in advance. If the articles are silent on the point, it would be perfectly in order for the proxy to present the form at the door of the meeting. However, it is usually thought preferable to receive the forms in advance so that they may be scrutinised before the meeting.

In contrast, articles rarely require a corporation appointing a representative to provide evidence in advance, and it is therefore perfectly in order for representatives to present their authority at the door of the meeting.

Articles can also specify the address where proxies are to be deposited. Table A specifies: 'at the office or at such other place . . . as is specified in the notice'. 'The notice' is the notice of the meeting. 'The office' is the registered office of the company, but the additional words are convenient to allow proxies to be sent, for example, to the registration department, or to the auditors' office if they are to act as tellers.

Some companies, on receipt of proxies, simply set them aside and ignore them on the basis that they are always there to be counted in the unlikely event of a poll. Where all business is non-contentious, this may seem safe; indeed, in the cost-conscious company it can be commended.

This carries risks, however. A poll can be demanded without warning and a good chairman will not wish to appear unprepared. In any event, knowledge of the number of votes covered by proxies can give a feeling of reassurance, and may make it possible to divert the demand for a poll. For all these reasons it is usually thought best to check each proxy, mark the number of shares held, analyse the votes for and against each resolution and prepare a summary for the chairman at the meeting.

Note must be taken of the cut-off time – usually 48 hours before the meeting. Proxies received late must not be counted. This can present problems if the meeting is held early in the week so that the latest time for lodging proxies is, say, midday on Sunday. Unless special arrangements can be made, it is usual to exclude proxies delivered by post on Monday morning but to include any that appear to have been delivered by hand over the weekend. Better still, the notice convening the meeting can specify that proxies may be deposited up to, say, first post Monday morning.

It will also be helpful to date-stamp the proxies on arrival. If any member sends in two or more proxies, the later will countermand the earlier, which should be excluded. Rejected proxies should be retained in case the vote is challenged.

If at the meeting a poll is demanded, a proxy will also be countermanded by any shareholder who votes in person. It is therefore desirable that the proxies should not only be counted but be sorted into alphabetical order for quick reference by the tellers at the meeting. Of course, if the register of members is held on computer, other and faster alternatives are available.

On a really contentious issue the opposition may circularise all, or some, shareholders independently, enclosing proxies of their own, usually worded to nominate not the chairman but someone of their own choice. Since they will have to do this at their own expense, there can be no objection to their selecting to whom they send proxy forms. Often they will ask for the proxy forms to be returned to their own address, usually 72 hours before the meeting. Since the period is not specified in the articles, this does not offend section 372(5) of the Act. The purpose of the different address and longer interval is of course to enable the opposition to assess the strength of their support before taking the proxies in bulk to the address specified in the notice.

Finally, on a highly contentious question, thought should be given to the merits of asking a professional firm such as the company's auditors (unless they are the source of the contention!) to act as tellers, checking and counting all proxies in advance of the meeting and subsequently checking and counting all votes on the poll. The objective is not so much to help the company's registrars at a time of great pressure (indeed, experience suggests that bringing in the auditors will only add to that pressure) but to present the result of the poll in a form which should satisfy even the most suspicious opposition.

If this course is adopted, the auditors should be given precise instructions by the secretary before they start work. Apart from points already made in this chapter, these might well include an instruction to refer to the company's solicitors any doubtful proxies and any the auditors believe they should reject.

Demanding a poll

As indicated earlier, voting must always be first by show of hands. Only when the chairman has declared the outcome of that first count may a poll be demanded.

Articles are void in so far as they do not provide minimum rights specified in section 373 of the Act. These are: (1) members have a statutory right to demand a poll at any general meeting on any question except the election of a chairman or the adjournment of the meeting; (2) a poll can be demanded by any five members entitled to vote; (3) alternatively, a poll can be demanded by members holding one-tenth of the voting rights at that meeting (or one-tenth of the paid-up capital conferring voting rights); and (4) a proxy may demand or join in demanding a poll.

Articles usually extend these minimum rights. For example, regulation 46 of Table A empowers the chairman to demand a poll and reduces the number of members required to demand a poll from five to two.

To take a poll voting papers are required. If a poll is expected, voting papers can be printed in advance, possibly in little tear-off books with a separate coloured sheet for each resolution. The danger is the unexpected demand for a poll, but the efficient company secretary will take to the meeting a supply of voting papers (which can conveniently be prepared on the office duplicator or photocopying machine) in a form suitable for any question on which a poll may be demanded.

In either form the minimum requirements for a voting paper are: (1) the number of the resolution being voted upon (which must of course correspond to the number used on the proxy forms); (2) the name of the person completing the form (in block capitals); (3) if a proxy, the name of the shareholder (also in block capitals); (4) the number of votes cast for the resolution; and (5) the votes cast against. On preprinted forms it may help to show the date of the meeting and also the actual wording of the resolution after the number at (1) above.

Other aspects of the procedure will be obvious. The chairman will first call for a show of hands, ask tellers to count, decide whether to use his casting vote and then declare the result. At that point (and only at that point) a poll may be demanded, either by the chairman or by the requisite number of members. After a quick check that the demand is adequate, the chairman should announce whether the poll will be taken immediately or, if not, when and where it will be taken.

Tellers should be appointed, either individuals (including at least one from each side) or a professional firm. Voting papers should then be distributed and receptacles (in an emergency an empty waste-paper basket or even a hat) indicated for collecting completed papers. Company staff will be expected to assist. If counting is expected to take some time, the chairman should announce when and where the result will be reported. This could be at an adjournment of the meeting, by a notice posted at the company's office, by post to every shareholder, or by press advertisement. He may also think it appropriate to announce when the ballot papers and proxy forms will be destroyed.

CHAPTER 7

Entitlement to vote

The right to vote depends not on the Act (which permits non-voting shares) but upon the company's articles of association.

Usually a company's articles deal very fully with voting rights and such related matters as proxies, representatives of corporate members and the procedure for taking a poll. Table A certainly covers all these points. As a last resort there are 'fall-back' provisions in section 370 of the Act which apply only where a particular point on voting and related matters is covered neither by Table A nor by special articles.

Occasionally voting rights, particularly for the holders of a special class of shares, will be governed not by the articles but by the terms on which those shares were issued. For example, regulation 54 of Table A, dealing with voting by members, commences: 'Subject to any rights or restrictions attached to any shares . . .'. This effectively brings such special terms of issue within the scope of the articles. Such a provision can be very inconvenient, however, requiring reference to an extra document which may not be readily available and may be overlooked, and so it is usually thought better to amend the articles to incorporate such special terms.

It may be helpful, before reading further, to refer to the table in Appendix C.

Joint shareholders

Where shares are held jointly, either holder may vote. If both vote, then only the vote of the senior should be counted, i.e. the vote of the person whose name appears first on the register. However, since a vote in person will always revoke a proxy, a vote in person by the second named would be counted in preference to a vote by proxy from the first named.

Both (or all) joint holders are members and so are entitled to attend the meeting, even though only one may vote. This can present obvious practical difficulties. How is the chairman to know that two persons in the body of the hall are joint holders and only one vote should be counted? It is not usually possible to separate joint holders, who may wish to sit together so that they may confer. One cannot treat the second named as a non-voter since he is entitled to vote if the first named does not. The use of voting cards may help, or if voting is close the problem may be resolved by someone demanding a poll. Sometimes joint holders split their shares into two or more holdings, each having one of the joint holders named first, thus solving the problem for the company as well as themselves.

Preference shareholders

There is nothing in the Act to say that preference shareholders (or any other class) shall or shall not vote at general meetings; it depends on the company's articles, or possibly on the terms of issue as explained above. If the shares are 'listed' on The Stock Exchange, one of the listing requirements is that preference shareholders shall be entitled to vote 'in appropriate circumstances'. They are in any event entitled to vote on any variation of their rights at a separate class meeting and this has been covered in Chapter 3.

So far as annual and extraordinary general meetings are concerned, a usual provision is that preference shareholders shall not vote except upon any matter where their rights are directly affected or if their cumulative preference dividends are in arrear, in which cases they may vote with the ordinary shareholders.

Those words 'directly affected' can be a pitfall. Consider a company having three classes of shares: 5% first preference, 9% second preference and ordinary. A proposal to increase the 5% first preference dividend to 6%, or to increase the authorised capital to permit the creation of more 5% first preference shares, clearly 'directly affects' the rights of the first preference holders; but it must not be overlooked that it also affects (and has been held to 'directly affect') the rights of the second preference holders. Indeed, it affects the rights of the ordinary holders as well. Whenever any change is proposed in the rights of one class of shareholders, it is therefore necessary to consider whether other classes are 'directly affected', bearing in mind the strict meaning the courts have attributed to those words.

As explained in Chapter 3, the procedure to vary class rights usually requires two or more meetings in quick succession in the same room. It is usually impracticable to exclude from one meeting a member who is entitled to vote only at another, especially as preference holders may be entitled to vote at the first and last of three or more meetings. The problem when counting votes will be obvious. Preference holders could be asked to enter by one door and sit on the left while ordinary holders enter by another and sit in the middle, but compliance cannot be guaranteed and many members may hold more than one class of share. Other problems arise if preference shareholders can vote on some but not all the business of an extraordinary general meeting.

Rather than seeking to manipulate the seating arrangements, therefore, it is better to issue voting cards of a different colour for each class. (Proxy cards of different colours can serve the same purpose if members are asked to bring them to the meeting, but it will be necessary to issue duplicates at the door to any who arrive after posting their proxies.) The chairman can then ask members to vote by holding up a card of the appropriate colour, while tellers can be instructed to ignore cards of the wrong colour.

Debenture holders

Holders of debenture stock and unsecured loan stock are not members and are not entitled to vote at general meetings. Any regulations for meetings of debenture holders will be found in the trust deed securing the stock.

Deceased members

It might appear obvious that a member who has died cannot vote; but consider a member who receives notice of a meeting, sends off a form of proxy, but dies before the meeting is held. His death revokes the proxy. This is a common-law rule, not to be found in the Act and rarely in articles of association, but binding nevertheless. When counting votes on a poll, care must therefore be taken to disregard votes cast by proxy for any member who has since died.

The question then arises: 'If the deceased can no longer vote, is there any other person who can vote in respect of his shares?'

Death of a joint holder

Articles almost invariably provide (as in regulation 29 of Table A) that on the death of a joint holder the shares devolve upon the survivor or survivors. Since the survivor is already registered in respect of the shares, no transfer, letter of request or even production of the death certificate is required to enable the survivor to vote in person or by proxy. Even if the deceased was the first-named holder, the survivor will automatically become 'the senior who tenders a vote' under regulation 55 or its equivalent.

Death of a sole holder

Where the deceased member held shares solely in his own name, regulation 30 of Table A provides that 'A person becoming entitled to a share in consequence of the death . . . of a member may, upon such evidence being produced as the directors may properly require, elect either to become the holder of the share or [to sign a transfer form]'.

The procedure is not automatic; if the executors or other legal personal representatives wish to vote, they must first produce 'such evidence . . . as the directors may properly require'. This will usually be probate of a will, letters of administration or (in Scotland) confirmation. Then they must 'elect . . . to become the holder', usually by completing a 'letter of request' asking for the shares to be registered in their own name(s). All this takes time and until the process is completed no one will be entitled to vote in respect of the shares held by the deceased. Indeed, the legal personal representatives will not even have the right to attend, although in practice an explanation of the circumstances will usually lead to an invitation to attend – but not vote.

Bankrupt members

The company is entitled to treat the registered holder as the only person entitled to any rights relating to the shares until it receives notice to the contrary. Accordingly it may recognise the vote of the bankrupt until formal evidence of bankruptcy is received, but, when a letter of request with evidence of title has been lodged, the trustee in bankruptcy may vote.

Shareholders resident abroad

Articles usually provide that a shareholder resident abroad is not entitled to notice of general meetings unless he has given the company an address in the United Kingdom to which such notices may be sent. However, this does not affect his right to attend and vote at the meeting as if he were resident in the UK.

However, a small but significant change in practice has arisen, almost unnoticed, under the Companies Act 1985 in relation to resolutions in writing. Under regulation 73A of 1948 Table A, a members' resolution in writing was valid if signed by all members 'entitled to receive notice'. Under regulation 53 of 1985 Table A, it must be signed by all members 'entitled to vote'. The signature of shareholders resident abroad is therefore required on a resolution in writing for a company governed by 1985 Table A, but not for a company governed by 1948 Table A.

Unpaid calls

Articles usually provide (as in regulation 57 of Table A) that a member shall not vote in respect of any share on which money is owing, e.g. for unpaid calls or overdue instalments.

Section 212 defaulters

Section 212 of the Act empowers a public company, *inter alia*, to require a member to disclose whether any other person has an interest in his shares. However, the section is not enforceable against a shareholder who is not resident in the United Kingdom. Some companies therefore take power in their articles to exclude from voting (and possibly also from entitlement to dividends) members to whom a section 212 notice has been issued but who have ignored it. Such a provision is perfectly valid, but in the case of a 'listed' company Stock Exchange regulations require such disenfranchisement to take effect not earlier than 28 days after service of notice. Such a provision seems reasonable for any company, 'listed' or not.

Representative of a corporate shareholder

A shareholder which is itself a company or other body corporate may vote either by completing a form of proxy or by appointing a representative under section 375 of the Act. This right is extended by section 740 to oversea companies, but it does not extend to a corporation sole.

A form of proxy is usually preferred because it is quick and simple. It does not require a board meeting, or the use of the seal. The formalities for completing a form of proxy are covered in Chapter 6.

However, a proxy has the right only to attend and vote on a poll. He cannot vote on a show of hands. At a meeting of a private company a proxy also has the right to speak (section 372(1) of the Act), but in the case of a public company a proxy is not entitled to speak. It follows that a proxy cannot demand (or join in demanding) a poll; if no one else demands a poll, a proxy has no vote. For this reason it is recommended that, if a corporate shareholder wishes a person of its own choice to attend the meeting, it should appoint him not as its proxy but as its representative under section 375 of the Act.

The relevant part of section 375 reads:

'A corporation, whether or not a company within the meaning of this Act, may . . . by resolution of its directors or other governing body authorise such persons as it thinks fit to act as its representative at any meeting of the company or at any meeting of any class of members of the company. . . . A person so authorised is entitled to exercise the same powers on behalf of the corporation which he represents as that corporation could exercise if it were an individual shareholder . . . of the other company.'

The words omitted extend this right to meetings of creditors, including debenture holders.

It will be seen that the right to appoint a representative is given by the Act itself. It does not depend on the company's articles of association.

A representative has far greater powers than a proxy. He can 'exercise the same powers . . . as that corporation could exercise if it were an individual shareholder'. Thus he can speak as well as vote, he can demand or join in demanding a poll and he can appoint a proxy in the name of the corporation which appointed him, in case he is unable to attend.

The appointment of a representative requires the formality of a board resolution, which might typically read:

'That Mr Brown, the Secretary of Shareholding Company p.l.c. ("the company"), be and is hereby appointed the company's representative under section 375 of the Companies Act 1985 to attend and vote for and in the name of the company at the Annual General Meeting of Subsidiary Limited to be held on 1st December 1986 and at any adjournment thereof.'

However, this procedure can be a little cumbersome if shares are held in several companies and separate board resolutions have to be passed on each occasion. It is therefore common practice to word the resolution so that it applies: (1) to any future meeting; and (2) to any (unnamed) company in which shares are held; and (3) not just to a named individual, but to a selection of individuals in the alternative, e.g. 'Mr A, or in his absence Mr B, or in his absence . . .', etc. This may even be extended to 'any person nominated in writing by the chairman'.

Putting all these ideas into a composite resolution, the board of the shareholding company might resolve:

'That the Secretary for the time being of Shareholding Company p.l.c. ("the company") or such other person as may be nominated by the Chairman [*or* by the Managing Director] of the company be and is hereby appointed the company's representative under section 375 of the Companies Act 1985 to attend and vote for and in the name of the company at any meeting of any other company in which the company holds shares or of which the company is a creditor with authority to exercise all powers of the company at such meeting and at any adjournment thereof, including the appointment of proxies.'

Nominees

Problems sometimes arise when a beneficial owner has his shares registered in the name of a trustee or nominee. There are many perfectly justifiable reasons for such an arrangement: absence overseas, security for a debt, convenience of administration or investment for a minor, for example. Often the beneficial owner will wish to vote in person and the nominee (the registered holder of the shares) will be agreeable, but how is this to be arranged?

The company's position is governed by its articles which invariably extend section 360 of the Act by including a provision similar to regulation 5 of Table A: '. . . the company shall not be bound by or recognise any interest in any share except an absolute right to the entirety thereof in the holder.' Hence, only the registered holder can vote unless (as in the event of death, bankruptcy, etc.) the articles or the law specifically provide otherwise.

However, the nominee has two obvious courses of action. It could appoint the beneficial owner as its proxy or (assuming, as is usual, that the nominee is a company) as its representative under section 375.

These alternatives are simple enough when the nominee represents only one beneficial owner or when all the beneficial owners wish to vote in the same way. Problems arise if one nominee represents several beneficiaries and they wish to vote different ways – or all wish to speak (possibly at length) at the meeting.

Any member may appoint more than one proxy to vote at the same meeting. This right may be inferred from section 372(2)(b) of the Act and the Interpretation Act 1978, but it does not extend to private companies unless the articles so provide. However, for a public company, the nominee can appoint each beneficial holder as a proxy, making it clear on each form of proxy how many votes that proxy is entitled to cast.

Alternatively, section 374 of the Act permits a member (and therefore a proxy for a member) on a poll to use only some of his votes, or to use some for and some against the same proposal. Thus the nominee can complete one form of proxy and indicate how many votes the proxy is to cast for or against each resolution. On an ordinary resolution it may be sufficient to cast a net number of votes, but on a special or extraordinary resolution the total 'for' and the total 'against' must both be completed, since any attempt to net the figures will upset the arithmetic in reckoning the three-fourths majority.

If a nominee holding shares for more than one beneficial holder appoints a representative, there appears to be no reason why it should not appoint as many representatives as there are beneficiaries. This rests not on the Act itself but upon the Interpretation Act 1978, which provides, *inter alia*, that unless the contrary is clearly indicated the singular includes the plural and vice versa. Hence, if a corporation can appoint one representative under section 375, then it can appoint more than one.

However, consider the problem if a large corporate shareholder has appointed some fifty or more representatives, each authorised to vote in respect of 100 shares – an obvious attempt to 'pack' the meeting.

The voting consequences can be neuturalised; if a solid block of fifty representatives votes against the motion, the chairman can demand a poll. But what if each representative in turn demands the right to speak on a particular question? Should they be allowed to delay the progress of the meeting? Faced with this situation some years ago, a chairman allowed the first representative of a corporate shareholder to speak at considerable length, but, as he sat down and the next representative of the same shareholder rose, the chairman pointed out that each *member* was entitled to speak once only and thus the first speaker had exhausted that right for that shareholder. His decision was probably not beyond challenge, but on that occasion it worked dramatically, to the great relief of the rest of the meeting.

CHAPTER 8

Problems with dates

Every company must hold an annual general meeting every year. Every company must also prepare annual accounts and lay these before the company in general meeting. These are two quite separate duties, but in practice most companies find it convenient to combine them, laying the annual accounts before the annual general meeting, which is held at about the same time each year.

Occasionally difficulties can arise, e.g. during early years before the regular annual routine is established, or if the company changes its accounting reference date or if the accounts are not ready in time.

In these circumstances it is necessary to go back to first principles, to consider what range of dates is practicable and permissible, first for the annual general meeting and then for laying the accounts before a general meeting (which need not be the annual general meeting), before deciding how best to resolve any conflict.

The date of the annual general meeting

The rules here are relatively simple:

1. Provided the first annual general meeting is held within 18 months of incorporation, no annual general meeting is required in the year a company is incorporated or in the following year.
2. Subject to that, every company must hold one annual general meeting, and only one, in each calendar year.
3. Every annual general meeting after the first must be held within 15 months after the previous one.

Accounting reference date

The date for laying the accounts before the company in general meeting and for filing a copy of the accounts with the Registrar of Companies is reckoned from the end of the accounting reference period. The following rules apply:

1. The directors may decide the accounting reference date for the company by board resolution and by filing form 224 with the Registrar of Companies, all within 6 months of incorporation.

2. If form 224 is not filed within 6 months, then the accounting reference date for that company will be 31st March.
3. The directors may change the accounting reference date (subject to certain limitations set out in section 225 of the Act) by board resolution and filing form 225(1).

   Any change will normally take effect on the *next* accounting reference date, and so it may be necessary to file one more set of accounts up to the old date, but there is one exception. If a subsidiary changes its date to conform to that of its holding company, or vice versa, and provided it files form 225(2) instead of 225(1) not later than the date for delivering the accounts to the Registrar of Companies, then the change can take immediate effect.
4. The accounting reference period is the period from one accounting reference date to the next. The financial year (i.e. the year covered by one set of accounts) commences on the day after the end of the last financial year and may end up to 7 days before or after the accounting reference date in the next year.

   Note that the accounting reference date and the accounting reference period will be the same in each year after the first. The dates are fixed; only the financial year can vary by a few days. Thus the accounting reference date could be fixed at 31st March, but, to suit accounting requirements or to facilitate stocktaking, the financial year could end on the last Saturday of March in each year.

Dates for laying and filing accounts

The rules are as follows:

1. The general rule is that accounts must be laid before the company in general meeting within 7 months for a public company or 10 months for a private company after the end of the accounting reference period. (NB: *not* after the end of the financial year).
2. The first accounting reference period of a new company runs from the day of incorporation to an accounting reference date between 6 and 18 months later. If the period is less than 12 months, the usual rules apply so that the accounts must be laid within 7 or 10 months. However, if the first accounting period is more than 12 months, the period for laying the accounts is shortened so that the last date for laying the accounts becomes 3 months after the end of the accounting reference period or, if later, 19 months (public company) or 22 months (private company) after incorporation.
3. However, a company which carries on business or has interests outside the United Kingdom, the Channel Islands and the Isle of Man may claim a three-month extension by filing form 242 with the Registrar of Companies *within* the original period (7 or 10 months) allowed for filing. The extension is valid for one year only; if overseas interests continue, filing form 242 must become part of the annual routine.

4. Overriding all this is a Stock Exchange requirement that a company whose shares are 'listed' must issue its annual report and accounts within 6 months of the end of the period to which they relate. However, the Stock Exchange requirement to *issue* the accounts (normally with notice of the meeting) within 6 months does not differ greatly from the statutory requirement to lay them before the company in general meeting within 7 months, when allowance is made for the statutory 21 clear days' notice.
5. A copy of the accounts must be delivered to the Registrar of Companies (with a translation if any part of it is not in English) within the same time limit as for laying the accounts before a general meeting. If the meeting is held in good time, it may be possible to file the accounts when filing the annual return, but, if the meeting is not held until the last few weeks within the permitted period, it may be necessary to file the accounts separately around the same date as the meeting.

Conflict of dates

No problems will arise if a company can repeat a well-established annual programme of dates. Accounts will be laid before the annual general meeting in good time and will be filed with the Registrar of Companies between two and six weeks after the meeting, with the annual return. Note, however, that if the accounts are to be filed at the same time as the annual return (and if a waiver of the statutory 21 clear days' notice is not practicable) notices of the annual general meeting with copies of the accounts must be sent to members five or six weeks before the end of the time limit for laying and filing accounts.

In unusual circumstances, however, such as the three cases outlined at the beginning of this chapter, it may be necessary to make separate arrangements for: (1) an annual general meeting at which no accounts will be available but following which the annual return will be filed; (2) an extraordinary general meeting to receive the accounts; and (3) filing the accounts separately from the annual return.

The starting-point for resolving any difficulties must be separate calculations to ascertain the earliest and latest practicable and permissible dates for holding the annual general meeting and for laying and delivering the accounts. It may be necessary to check against each of the numbered paragraphs in the previous sections of this chapter, considering all possibilities.

Typically it may be found that the annual general meeting can be held at any time between 2nd January (since 1st January is a bank holiday) and 15 months after the last annual general meeting, while the range of dates for the accounts may commence when the auditors have signed their report and end 7, 10 or 13 months after the accounting reference date. If these two ranges of dates overlap, the accounts can be laid before an annual general meeting held within the overlap. It will also be necessary to file the accounts with the Registrar of Companies within the overlap.

If the ranges of dates do not overlap, separate meetings will be necessary: an annual general meeting to comply with section 366(1) of the Act and another meeting to present the accounts. This second meeting will probably be an extraordinary general meeting. However, bearing in mind that accounts can be laid and filed up to 13 months after the accounting reference date, it could, in some circumstances, be the annual meeting for the following year.

If the difficulty in matching dates arises from a change in the accounting reference date, it may be necessary to work through a programme of two, three or even four years of holding separate meetings before it is possible to lay accounts before an annual general meeting. It may be best to plan for several years ahead to minimise the 'out-of-phase' period.

Business at a separate annual general meeting

No particular problems arise if the accounts can be presented at an annual general meeting. The usual business will be found in the draft notice for an annual general meeting in Appendix G. However, if separate meetings are required, the question must arise: 'What business can be done at an annual general meeting where there are no accounts?'

Often the answer is 'None!' The meeting must be duly convened and held, the chairman must check that a quorum is present, he may then say a few words about the progress of the business, but he need not even do that. It will then be his duty to close the meeting.

This odd situation arises because, while the Act requires every company to hold an annual general meeting each year, it does not specify any business to be conducted at that meeting. However, before concluding that there will be no business for such a meeting, it would be prudent to examine the company's articles and also the minutes of meetings during the previous year.

Articles often require one-third of the directors to retire in rotation at the conclusion of the annual general meeting; they may then offer themselves for re-election at the annual general meeting. The previous year's resolution appointing or reappointing auditors will often provide that they shall hold office until the next annual general meeting. Auditors' or directors' remuneration may also be dependent on a resolution which can only be passed (or may more conveniently be passed) at the annual general meeting.

There is a growing practice of wording articles and resolutions so that such business is done not at the annual general meeting but at 'the next meeting before which accounts are laid'. This has much to commend it.

Default

Occasionally default becomes inevitable. In this event the Department of Trade and Industry has power under section 367 of the Act to direct the calling of an annual general meeting and to give ancillary directions which could include, for example, that one person (or one proxy) shall constitute a valid meeting. It could also fix a date outside the statutory limits.

Annual return

As we have seen, the accounts must be filed with the Registrar of Companies within the same time limit as that for laying the accounts. The annual return, however, must be filed within 42 days after the *annual* general meeting, whether or not accounts were laid before that meeting. The obligations to file accounts and to file the annual return, although often fulfilled on the same date, are in fact separate obligations which may have to be honoured on different dates.

CHAPTER 9

Practical aspects

The formal and legal background to any company meeting has been covered by the preceding chapters. Our purpose now is to bring together into chronological sequence all the practical aspects of convening and conducting a successful meeting. In doing this we shall bear in mind that, while 99 per cent of company meetings are routine and uneventful, one must always be prepared for difficulties and these can arise when least expected.

We shall take as our example a public limited company with 'listed' shares (i.e. with shares or other securities listed on The Stock Exchange) which is about to call a general meeting (be it an annual general meeting or extraordinary general meeting) before which the accounts will be laid and which will therefore deal with all annual items such as a dividend and re-election of directors and auditors. For good measure we shall include in the business a special resolution. Thus, by including everything special, we shall cover every variety of simpler meeting.

Appendices D to F comprise a series of preliminary 'checklists', while Appendices G to K offer a draft notice, chairman's notes (or 'extended agenda'), draft minutes and a form of proxy for a general meeting. Appendix L presents a selection of ordinary and special resolutions. For the simpler meeting, items which do not apply can readily be ignored.

Timetable of work

It is first advisable to prepare a timetable listing all items requiring attention, with a view to ensuring that nothing is overlooked and all relevant time limits are observed. An outline for such a timetable will be found in Appendix D.

Two dates are critical and must be settled at the outset. First is the date of the board meeting at which the directors will consider the accounts, and this will primarily depend upon the date which the auditors can indicate (with confidence!) for completion of the audit. An additional seven days at least should be allowed for circulation of the draft accounts to the directors with notice of the board meeting.

The second critical date is that of the general meeting itself. Allowance must be made for the printers' 'lead time' from the point, immediately after the board meeting, when they receive the typed draft accounts with all supporting material, until they post the printed accounts to all shareholders, plus about 25 days to meet statutory requirements.

The 'Continuing Obligations' for 'listed' companies reinforce the Company Securities (Insider Dealing) Act 1985 by requiring them to adopt a code of conduct for their directors at least as strict as the Stock Exchange Model Code, which requires, *inter alia*, a 'close period' of two months before the announcement of profits or other price-sensitive information during which neither directors nor their families or associates may buy or sell the company's securities.

Accordingly, as soon as a decision has been reached on the date of the board meeting to agree the profit announcement, it would be appropriate to notify directors of the date the 'close season' commences – or that it has already begun, if that is the case.

When the dates of the board meeting and general meeting have been settled – and agreed with the chairman – there should be no difficulty in completing the rest of the timetable with the aid of Appendix D.

Selecting and preparing the room

The choice of a room for the general meeting may sometimes be obvious – the company's boardroom may be judged large enough, a hotel company may have an eminently suitable room, or a shipping company may choose the dining-saloon of its cruise liner not so much because of its suitability for a general meeting but more for the advertising value of inviting shareholders to sample the luxuries aboard.

In most cases, however, a p.l.c. with 'listed' shares will wish to rent a suitable room, possibly at a convenient hotel, but in all circumstances the checklist in Appendix E should prove useful in considering suitability and checking the availability of all necessary facilities.

Since it is impossible to forecast attendance with any degree of accuracy, seating capacity should be well in excess of numbers expected. Previous experience may indicate the likely attendance, but it is usually found that the first annual general meeting after flotation as a public company is better attended than subsequent meetings, while bad news (such as a sharp downturn in profits, a contentious merger or anything that suggests a change of direction) will invariably mean a larger attendance.

It is prudent to err on the side of caution not only in terms of numbers but also as regards time. Most general meetings are over within a few minutes so that it may seem extravagant to hire a room for a full half a day or longer. However, there is nothing quite so exasperating, for chairman and shareholders alike, as finding that an unexpected number of questions or deliberate filibustering on a contentious issue necessitates adjournment of the meeting for no better reason than that a queue at the door is demanding admission to a later meeting. Moreover, time to spare, after the formal business, for a leisurely chat with press and shareholders can have considerable public relations value.

The time of the meeting may not be significant in most cases, but if an important statement is to be made, or if contentious matters will be discussed, thought must be given to the possibility that after an early meeting the evening papers may carry an incomplete report, stealing thunder from the company's own prepared (and possibly embargoed) statement for the following morning's press.

When the date and time have been fixed and the room selected, commercial prudence dictates that all requirements should be listed in a letter to the hotel management. In any case it is strongly recommended that the secretary or someone deputed by him should arrive two or three hours before the meeting (possibly the previous evening) to see that all requirements have been met. Unless access is obvious, this inspection should include a walk from the car park and also from the point at which taxis and other public transport will set down passengers, as this will enable one to consider the impression a stranger will gain, to ensure that adequate direction notices are in place and to check that hotel reception and other staff have been given sufficient instruction to give prompt guidance to shareholders who ask the way.

The board meeting

Before the general meeting is called, the report and accounts must be considered by the directors, normally at a board meeting although some very small companies may substitute a written resolution signed by all the directors as explained in Chapter 10.

For a 'listed' company, The Stock Exchange must be notified in advance of the date of any board meeting which is expected to decide on (or recommend) a dividend or any announcement of profits or losses for the year, half-year or any other period.

The minimum agenda for this board meeting is to approve the profit and loss account and authorise two directors to sign the balance sheet, to comply with sections 238(4) and 238(1) respectively of the Act. In practice the meeting will also consider the report and accounts as a whole, the dividend to be recommended and any related matters.

It cannot be stressed too strongly that, for a 'listed' company, everything comprised in the report and accounts must at this stage be treated as highly confidential – particularly the profits and proposed dividend, but with inexperienced staff it is safer to say 'everything'. As to what constitutes the 'report and accounts', see page 53.

Notice of the board meeting should be given in accordance with the usual practice. At least seven days' notice is usual, and the notice and agenda should be accompanied by copies of the report and accounts which the directors are to consider. Envelopes should be marked 'Confidential'.

The auditors are usually invited to attend this board meeting not as a legal right or necessity but for the convenience of the directors if questions arise. Moreover, it should ensure the auditors' agreement – or at least acquiescence – to decisions reached, and provide an opportunity for asking them to sign their report at the earliest opportunity. The prudent secretary will, however, ensure that another room is available nearby in case the directors ask the auditors to retire while they discuss any point of difficulty.

In any event it must be remembered – and it may be useful to remind the directors – that the accounts are the directors' accounts. While the auditors may have much to contribute, on any point of difference the directors have the last word. The only power of the auditors is to qualify the auditors' report, but experience shows that, while some auditors will threaten to do this on trivialities, in practice they invariably climb down unless a major point of principle is involved.

If directors retire by rotation, the meeting will usually settle who should retire on this occasion. Articles usually provide (as in regulation 74 of Table A) that, if two directors were last reappointed on the same day, they shall agree which shall retire first, or failing agreement the matter shall be settled by lot. Either way the matter is best resolved at the board meeting and recorded in the minutes.

On dividends, articles usually provide (e.g. regulations 103 and 102 respectively of Table A) that the directors may declare and pay interim dividends but may only *recommend* a final dividend which is then declared by the general meeting subject to the proviso that the dividend so declared must not exceed the rate recommended by the directors. To resolve possible uncertainty or to avoid timing problems, the directors will sometimes declare and pay a 'second interim' dividend (which does not require shareholders' approval) and then recommend that no final dividend be paid.

At the same board meeting the secretary should be formally authorised to issue the documents and to call the general meeting at a specified place, date and time.

At the conclusion of the meeting:

1. Two directors should sign the balance sheet.
2. They should also sign any consolidated balance sheet.
3. The secretary should sign the directors' report.
4. The auditors, if present, should sign their report.
5. The preliminary announcement should be sent to The Stock Exchange.
6. The notice of the meeting and the report and accounts (see below) should be sent to the printers.

Preliminary announcement

A public company wishing to have its shares 'listed' on The Stock Exchange will be required to enter into certain undertakings including the 'Continuing Obligations' which comprise a number of extra-statutory regulations prescribed by The Stock Exchange. These rules cover a range of activities not all of which relate to meetings, but of particular relevance in the present context is the requirement to make, as soon as the board has considered the draft accounts, a 'preliminary announcement' of the results and dividend for the year. Until this announcement has been made, the figures must be treated as confidential. Once the preliminary announcement has been received by The Stock Exchange, the need for confidentiality expires and the figures can safely be put into the hands of the press and printers.

The preliminary profit statement should contain the following information in tabular form, with comparative figures for the corresponding previous period:

1. Net turnover.
2. Profit or loss before tax and extraordinary items.
3. Tax on profits (distinguishing UK tax and if material showing overseas tax separately).
4. Minority interests.
5. Profit or loss attributable to shareholders, before extraordinary items.
6. Extraordinary items, net of tax.
7. Profit or loss attributable.
8. Rates of dividend paid or proposed and amounts absorbed thereby.
9. Earnings, expressed as pence per share.

Half-yearly report

The Stock Exchange regulations also require every 'listed' company to issue a half-yearly profit statement within four months after the end of the first six months of its financial year. The figures to be included are the same as for the annual preliminary statement, so far as applicable, and in addition if the half-yearly figures are unaudited the statement should say so. The report must either be sent to all holders of listed securities or be inserted as a paid advertisement in two national daily newspapers. The procedures for ensuring confidentiality until the statement is issued to The Stock Exchange immediately after the board meeting are the same as for the annual statement.

Annual report and accounts

The report and accounts comprise:

1. Profit and loss account.
2. Balance sheet.
3. The directors' report.
4. The auditors' report.
5. Group accounts, if the company has subsidiaries. These normally comprise:

   (a) consolidated balance sheet *in addition to* the company's own (unconsolidated) balance sheet;
   (b) consolidated profit and loss account *instead of* the company's own profit and loss account.

   According to circumstances, group accounts can be presented in other ways, as specified in section 229(6) of the Act.

The most voluminous part of the report and accounts in practice will usually be the notes on the accounts, but as these are in fact part of the profit and loss account, balance sheet and consolidated balance sheet they have not been listed separately here.

Bound within the same covers will usually be found these items:

6. Notice of the general meeting;
7. The chairman's statement;
8. Additional material of an advertising or public relations character. Practice varies, but the trend towards presenting this in a separate (matching?) booklet to be sent to shareholders in the same envelope as the report and accounts has much to commend it.

Style of presentation

The precise style of presentation is a matter of taste and is often left to design consultants, but a few general propositions merit consideration.

A4 size is so usual as to be almost imperative. It cannot be in the company's interest to produce an odd-sized booklet which investors have difficulty in filing and therefore in finding.

Many shareholders, and more particularly investment analysts who often influence investors, will wish to make notes or calculations in the margins alongside the figures. Paper that will take both pencil and ball-point without smudging is therefore desirable.

The order of items within the booklet also merits careful thought. It can be argued that the notice of the meeting should appear first since all other items depend upon it. Others would argue that very few members attend the meeting or even send proxies, and so the accounts should take priority. The chairman or public relations consultants may offer rival claims. The best advice is that the first page on opening should present a short table of contents so that each reader may readily find whatever it is that he regards as most important.

Since a table of contents will not require a full page, the rest can usefully be occupied by a summary of the year's results including (particularly) an announcement of the dividend. A dividend announcement is incomplete unless it gives, in addition to the rate of dividend in pence per share, both the date it will be paid and the record date. Many shareholders will look for the dividend announcement first, but find incomplete information scattered throughout the booklet. The 'contents' page provides an opportunity to bring all dividend information together where it can readily be found.

Preparations on the day of the meeting

Mention has already been made of the advisability of inspecting the room (and access to the room) well before the time fixed for the meeting, checking that all is prepared. It may be convenient to do this with the aid of Appendices E and F, checking that everything is in order and that all necessary documents are to hand.

An adequate number of stewards can welcome persons arriving and direct them to a table (possibly one of several) to sign an attendance sheet. Usually separate sheets are provided: (1) for members and their proxies; (2) for the press; and (3) for others.

The press will usually be provided with seats at a table convenient for their notebooks. If, expecting trouble, the company has engaged a shorthand writer (better in these circumstances than a tape recorder, since speakers may wave a microphone aside or may refuse to give their names, in which event a shorthand writer can at least include a brief description), he can be seated at the press table, but will usually prefer a small table to himself, *facing* the assembled shareholders.

Clear instructions should be given for dealing with persons having no entitlement to attend. Neither possession of a proxy card nor a copy of the accounts is evidence of membership. It may be necessary to deal firmly with determined gatecrashers, attracted possibly by the offer of refreshments at the end of the meeting. On the other hand, stockbrokers, bankers and others having a genuine interest in the proceedings should obviously be admitted. Friends and relatives of shareholders (such as a husband purporting to represent his wife, or vice versa) will usually be admitted but may need to be reminded that (unless duly appointed as proxy) they are not entitled to vote. Indeed, they may be asked to sit separately to facilitate counting votes.

It will be essential in dealing with difficult cases to have access to a list of members. This could comprise either the register itself or the dividend list. If the register is maintained by computer, a portable terminal with an open line to the registration office is an obvious convenience. At worst, a telephone should be available. Some companies sent out attendence cards as well as proxy cards, but these are probably worse than useless since they can encourage and (except in cases of 'husband for wife') actually facilitate impersonation.

The resolution to reappoint the auditors and to fix their remuneration is usually thought better proposed from the body of the meeting rather than by a director. If the draft resolution is typed on a small card, one of the stewards can ask a shareholder on arrival to make the formal proposal in suitable terms. If possible, his name (on another, similar card?) should be passed to the secretary for inclusion in the chairman's notes.

Platform arrangements will be at the discretion of the chairman. He will usually wish all the directors to be seated at the table, with the secretary and possibly the company's solicitors; the chief accountant, too, may be asked to sit nearby. Often auditors are asked to sit on the platform but will usually decline, preferring to sit in the body of the hall to emphasise that they are appointed by and report to the shareholders rather than the board.

When it has been decided who is to sit at the top table, it would help to use 'place markers' and circulate a seating plan before the meeting.

Everyone on the top table should be provided with a notepad and pencil or ball-point pen, and also a copy of the report and accounts. Sometimes they are provided with a copy of the memorandum and articles, but it is usually thought sufficient to leave one or two copies in the centre of the table where they can be referred to if necessary.

Selected employees may be invited to attend. This is good employee relations. Requests for 'time off' to attend can best be met by a suggestion that a small number of employee-shareholders be chosen by their colleagues to attend and report back. It can be good public relations, too, if employees (whether or not shareholders) can mingle with others before and after the meeting. A few carefully selected employees can also be a useful safeguard if difficulties arise.

The chairman's notes or extended agenda

The secretary, and possibly the chairman, too, should have a copy of the memorandum and articles and also a copy of the Companies Act, both with a good index for quick reference. An argument in the middle of the meeting is no time for lengthy searching for some minor but necessary detail. An indexed copy of the Act is available commercially, while a competent clerk could prepare an index to the articles in an hour or so.

Of prime importance, however, are the chairman's detailed notes or, as they are sometimes termed, the chairman's extended agenda.

The main purpose of such notes is not just to amplify the necessarily brief outline of the business set out in the notice but to ensure that procedural points are not overlooked. Thus the chairman should be advised what quorum is required and reminded to check that it is present before commencing business, should be reminded that a three-fourths majority is required for a special or extraordinary resolution, should be reminded of the precise procedure for demanding a poll or handling a demand from the floor of the meeting, and should be aware who is entitled to vote (by a copy, perhaps, of the table in Appendix C) so that he can give an immediate authoritative ruling to any point raised. Such questions may rarely arise, but, if a meeting 'turns difficult', success or otherwise will often depend upon the care taken earlier in preparing the chairman's notes.

If the chairman's notes are too brief, they may well be inadequate; if too verbose, they may defeat their objective since it may be difficult to find reference to the point at issue. While much depends on the experience and temperament of the chairman, even more depends on the skill of the secretary – not just in providing all that is required (and no more), but in laying out the notes and cross-referencing them so that any point arising can be found quickly.

Draft chairman's notes will be found in Appendix H, but these present only one style and may not suit all chairmen. An experienced chairman may need no more than a brief heading for each item suggesting who should be called upon to propose and second each resolution. Most will wish to have at least the draft wording for each resolution. Some may require very full notes amounting to a complete verbatim draft written in the style of a play-script, showing every word to be said, with alternatives to cover, for example, a declaration that a resolution has been carried on a show of hands or suitable wording for demanding a poll.

The secretary should, of course, have a copy of the chairman's notes before him at the meeting. Indeed, it is sometimes suggested that every director should have a copy. However, this can be counter-productive. It can be disconcerting to shareholders if fifteen directors on the top table all turn a page at the same moment. More important, a director who has to speak only once to propose or second a resolution can easily miss his cue if trying to follow the meeting through pages of typescript; he will do better to follow by listening and waiting for the moment when, called by the chairman, he can pick up and read from one sheet bearing just the words he is required to say.

Beyond that, the draft chairman's notes in Appendix G should be self-explanatory, but one point may need stressing. For a 'listed' company, one of the 'Continuing Obligations' under Stock Exchange regulations is to avoid creating a false market in the company's securities, a position where one party buying or selling shares has an unfair advantage over another because he has earlier access to information released by the company. It is therefore desirable to avoid saying at the meeting (e.g. in answer to a shareholder's question) anything that is 'price-sensitive' unless it has already been released generally, e.g. in the report and accounts. If this cannot be avoided, or if something slips out inadvertently, The Stock Exchange should be informed at once. A formal press release may also be desirable.

The secretary who has prepared or the chairman who has read and understood detailed chairman's notes on the lines of Appendix H should have no difficulty with any points likely to arise at the meeting.

Quorum

The requirement for a quorum rarely presents problems at the general meeting of a p.l.c. Table A, for example (regulation 40), requires a quorum of two persons entitled to vote, and special articles seldom require more than three or five. There are usually at least such a number of directors who are also shareholders and who will therefore provide the quorum.

At a general meeting, shareholders do not have to be disregarded in counting the quorum on the grounds that they may have a financial interest in the subject under discussion. The rules applying to directors do not apply to shareholders.

Difficulties may arise at class meetings, where the requirement is larger, or for the smaller private company where it may be difficult to get even two shareholders together for a meeting, but such cases have been covered fully in Chapter 3.

After the meeting

After the meeting it will be the duty of the secretary to write up the minutes and to ensure that all decisions of the meeting are carried out. Payment of the dividend may be top priority and require a phone call to the company's registrar immediately after the meeting, but other matters can usually be left

articles. Table A requires a quorum of two directors, but a more usual provision for a p.l.c. is at least half the directors. A problem unique to board meetings is whether a director precluded from voting because he has a fiduciary interest in the proceedings can be counted in the quorum. This depends on the articles and is discussed later.

Secretary

Every company must have a secretary who, in the case of a public company, must be suitably qualified under section 286 of the Act. The Act does not define the secretary's duties – perhaps Parliament thought these too obvious to require legislation. They are usually very wide-ranging, depending upon the size of company and nature of its business, but the importance of preparation for, attendance at and follow-up after board meetings must not be underestimated. The success of the board meeting may largely depend on the secretary's skill in arranging and presenting board papers, while the success of the business may depend on his skill in communicating the decisions and on his perseverence in ensuring they are implemented.

Notice

Articles usually provide (as in regulation 88 of Table A) that a director may, and the secretary at the request of a director shall, call a board meeting. In practice, board meetings are invariably called by the secretary, usually according to a prearranged programme but on occasion at the request of the chairman.

'Notice' of the meeting can refer to notification of the place, date and time; or it can refer to notice of the business to be conducted.

In the first sense, it is clearly important that every director should know where and when a board meeting is to be held. No period of notice is specified in the Act and it is unusual to find it in articles. Board procedure, including length of notice, is for the directors themselves to decide (regulation 88 of Table A, or its equivalent) and most companies fix a programme for at least a year at a time – say, the first Tuesday of each month at 2.30 p.m. at the registered office. If every director has been given such a timetable, there is no requirement to give separate notice of each meeting as the date approaches. A reminder may be good practice, but the agenda paper will usually serve this purpose.

If there is no such timetable and the directors give no indication of their expectations, then reasonable notice must be given. Seven days' notice should be adequate in most cases. Where notice is given, it must be given to all directors, even those who are known to be abroad or unwell or who have indicated that they will not attend. Oral notice is sufficient unless the articles require written notice.

In the other sense, there is, strictly speaking, no requirement to give notice of *the business* for a board meeting. Unlike shareholders, who may choose whether or not to attend a general meeting, directors have a duty to attend every board meeting irrespective of the business to be transacted.

It will be obvious, however, that, regardless of legal niceties, business will be expedited and better decisions are likely to be taken if every director has ample prior opportunity to consider the business, furnished with all relevant facts and arguments. Hence the usual practice is to circulate, at least seven days in advance, a detailed agenda paper listing the business for discussion, supported by reports from the managing director or other chief executive, from departmental managers and from those who wish to advocate board support for some policy or some course of action.

Such an agenda paper in no way limits the business of the meeting. Unlike a shareholder at a general meeting, no director, present or not, can complain if matters are raised which do not appear on the agenda. It may not be the best way of conducting business, but is otherwise unobjectionable.

While formal notice of a board meeting is not required if every director knows when and where it is to be held, this does not dispense with all formality. If all the directors happen to meet casually, then they can agree to turn the occasion into a board meeting; but some of the directors cannot insist on doing so if others object on the grounds of inadequate notice.

Preparing the agenda paper

Conduct of a board meeting is under the control of the directors, led by the chairman and guided by the secretary. Probably there are as many variations as there are public companies. Often the agenda paper will comprise a list of items: 'To consider the attached report dated . . . from . . . concerning . . .'. In addition there may be items needing no supporting papers.

The task of the secretary, or his assistant, will be to ensure that all reports and papers for consideration by the board are in his hands in good time, to list them in proper form on the agenda paper, to submit this in draft to the chairman and, subject to his approval, to circulate copies will all supporting papers to every director.

The order in which items are to be considered will be a matter of judgement. Matters arising from the last meeting, such as approval of the minutes or brief reports on implementation of decisions recorded in those minutes, will clearly come first. Matters looking forward to the next meeting, such as fixing the date (if not already agreed as part of a timetable) or a request for a particular matter to appear on the agenda, should logically appear at the end. The middle is likely to be occupied by weightier matters, possibly the subject of long reports. This arrangement has the advantage that anyone arriving a little late or leaving just before the end is unlikely to miss the more important items of business.

Thought must also be given to whether decisions on one subject are dependent on others. Management accounts usually appear early since most other items entail spending money, the availability of which may depend on the accounting results. Occasionally the order may be reversed – the accounts may be more meaningful if the board has some idea whether an overdraft can be negotiated or whether major expenditure will be sanctioned.

The secretary may on occasion have to draft board reports himself. His advice may also be sought by his colleagues, who, while excellent at their own jobs, will often be inexperienced in board procedure. The following suggestions may prove useful.

It is usually best to keep the agenda itself as short as possible, leaving detail to the supporting papers. This implies that every paper will set out clearly what decisions are required from the board. A list of recommendations often appears at the end of the report, though it may be thought better to put the recommendations first so that the reader can grasp at the outset what judgements are expected of him – judgements he will make, at least tentatively, as he reads the information and arguments which follow.

Thus every board paper should commence by stating why it has been prepared (e.g. at the request of the board and/or to make specific recommendations), set out those recommendations, continue by reciting the facts, marshalling all the arguments for and against, and conclude by listing the points upon which decisions are required. Detailed figures, cost or profit estimates, technical data, etc., are best set out in schedules to keep the paper itself as concise as possible.

A balanced paper will present all the arguments, whether favourable to the recommendations or otherwise. It may help the manager who doubts the value of this to consider that every member of the board will be looking for weaknesses, for some argument that has apparently been overlooked. It is better to include that counter-argument where there is an opportunity to comment upon it, rather than leave it to those who may form judgements on the basis of an apparent oversight.

Of course, having recited both sides of the case, the manager is entitled to offer the strongest support for his recommendations. If the board finds it necessary to decide against, it is unlikely to criticise a manager for having the courage of his convictions, while a good manager will loyally support the board decision whether or not it was what he recommended.

The secretary is in a very different position. Except where he is himself submitting a report in his other capacity of departmental manager, he will not be expected to take sides. His competence and efficiency as secretary will often depend on his ability to preserve at least the appearance of impartiality. This should be evident even in the way board papers are drafted (for example, agenda items should be worded 'To consider whether . . .' rather than 'To agree that . . .') and in the style in which the minutes are drafted (see later). This air of impartiality will prove invaluable when the secretary has to communicate and possibly enforce board decisions, or at least to check on action taken. In the extreme case of a boardroom split, his reputation for impartiality may save his job.

This practice of brief agenda items supported by more detailed papers can also be useful in unusual circumstances. For example, a director may write to the secretary or to the chairman: 'I think at the next board meeting we should discuss . . .'. Such a very general request can be difficult to express in the form of an agenda item, unless worded: 'To consider a letter (copy attached) from . . .

regarding . . .'. Similarly an oral request can appear on the agenda: 'To consider a proposal made orally by . . . that . . .'.

Board papers are sometimes described as 'tabled'. What does this mean? Originally the term meant 'laid upon the table'; when a paper under discussion was 'tabled', the discussion was ended.

Over the years the meaning seems to have changed. It is commonly used today to refer to papers made available to directors for background information but which require no decision or discussion. It can also be used to describe papers which should have been circulated with the agenda but, not being available until the last moment, are presented at the meeting, a practice any efficient organisation will of course try to avoid. The term 'tabled' has in fact become so ambiguous that it is better avoided.

However, this raises the question whether papers which give information but require no decisions should appear on the agenda at all. Sometimes they obviously should; the monthly management accounts, for example, may include no recommendations but be necessary background for decisions to be taken on later papers. In other cases, papers with no recommendations are probably best kept off the agenda, circulated for information rather than discussion.

The board meeting of a p.l.c. may cost well over £2 a minute in fees and salaries alone – perhaps double if all expenses are included. Such expenditure may be well worth while if it leads to important business decisions, but otherwise anything that saves board time saves money.

The first board meeting

The first board meeting of a company, while following all the rules, will be unusual in regard to its agenda in so far as it will include a number of items necessarily consequent on the incorporation of the company. Indeed, this can provide an interesting illustration of the need for logical order, to which reference has already been made. Typically the agenda for a company's first board meeting will include the following:

1. The secretary to report the incorporation of the company and to lay before the meeting a copy of the memorandum and articles.
2. To appoint a chairman.
3. To appoint additional directors.
4. To appoint alternate directors.
5. To appoint a managing director.
6. To adopt a common seal and to decide who may authorise its use.
7. To allot shares and seal share certificates.
8. To open an account at . . . . Bank p.l.c.
9. To appoint auditors.
10. To decide the accounting reference date.
11. To receive directors' declarations of interests.
12. To consider the attached report, dated . . ., from . . . relating to the company's intended business.

A few moments' reflection will show the logical order. Item 1 establishes that there is a company, without which there can be no meeting. Item 2 establishes that the meeting is duly constituted. (Form G10 filed when the company was formed will establish who are the first directors and who is the secretary. It is for the chairman to ensure there is a quorum.) Item 4 may depend on item 3. A common seal must be adopted before share certificates can be sealed, while as soon as shares are allotted it will be necessary to open a bank account for the allotment money, and so on.

Since this is the first board meeting, there will be no previous minutes. At every later meeting the first two items will normally be:

1. To receive the minutes of the last board meeting held on . . . and to authorise the chairman to sign them.
2. To consider any matters arising from these minutes.

Directors' interests in contracts

Under section 317 of the Act it is the duty of a director who is in any way, directly or indirectly, interested in a contract or proposed contract with the company to declare the nature of his interest at a board meeting. He must do this at the earliest opportunity. This is a statutory requirement which cannot be waived by the directors, by the articles or by the shareholders.

'Contract' and 'interest' are not defined in the Act, but 'contract' would include any agreement or arrangement which the company made or proposed with the director, with a member of his immediate family, or with a company or partnership of which he was a director or member. 'Interest' would include any arrangement conferring any financial advantage, however remote or contingent. While a trivial advantage could doubtless be ignored under the *de minimis* rule, it would probably be unsafe to ignore any interest on the grounds that it was too remote.

While the duty to 'declare his interest' rests with the director, most directors would doubtless appreciate a reminder and the secretary should bear in mind each director's outside interests (directorships, partnerships, etc.) with a view to tactfully prompting the director if necessary. In any event the secretary should, for the protection of the director, ensure that every disclosure of an interest is recorded in the minutes. A suitable draft wording will be found in Appendix M.

Section 317(3) permits a director to discharge his duty of disclosure by giving general notice that he is to be regarded as interested in any contract the company may make with a specified list of companies, partnerships and persons. This very convenient practice is also covered by the draft minutes in Appendix M.

Even when a director has disclosed his interest, since he is in a fiduciary position in relation to the company, he is at common law precluded from voting at a board meeting on or from making any profit, however indirect, from any contract with the company; but these rather stringent requirements may be softened by the articles.

Regulation 85 of Table A not only permits a director to be a party to any contract with the company, but also permits him to retain any profit arising from that contract. Regulation 94 of Table A provides that a director shall not vote on a contract in which he is interested if his interest is material and conflicts (or may conflict) with the interests of the company, but this is subject to certain exceptions relating to approved pension schemes, guarantees, indemnities and securities.

It must be emphasised, however, that this covers only a company subject to 1985 Table A. Regard must be paid to each company's own articles, or where relevant to Table A of the Companies Act under which it was incorporated. A company secretary should of course be familiar with his own company's articles on these important points.

In the case of a 'listed' company, The Stock Exchange requires the articles to include provision that a director shall not vote on any contract in which he has a material interest, subject to such exceptions as The Stock Exchange may approve.

A prohibition against voting could obviously give rise to difficulty. A board meeting which started with a quorum may reach an item of business in which a director has an interest and so the meeting may find itself without a quorum. The chairman has no choice but to proceed to the next business – or, if there is no more business, then to adjourn the meeting.

Regulation 98 of Table A empowers the chairman to decide any question of a director's right to vote. This can be useful, but must be used with care. The regulation is intended to deal with cases of real uncertainty and the chairman could not give a ruling in flagrant violation of the articles.

How, then, is the unfinished business to be completed? There are several alternatives. If the business is not urgent, it could wait until the next meeting in the hope that more directors may be present. It may be possible (and would certainly be permissible) to split the business. For example, if the board is considering the appointment of two directors to salaried appointments and therefore neither can vote, separate resolutions relating to each director would enable each to vote on the other appointment, restoring a quorum (admittedly a different quorum) for each item of business.

Finally, it may be possible, at least for a small company, to refer the matter to the shareholders. At a general meeting, every person entitled to vote – even if also a director – is entitled to consider only himself. He will not be precluded from voting by reason of any fiduciary interest.

Thus if the board reaches an impasse it can adjourn and convene a general meeting to deal with the unfinished business. With a very small company where the directors and shareholders are almost identical, the general meeting could be held (with appropriate waivers of notice) during a brief adjournment of the board meeting, which could then resume. Alternatively, if the articles so provide (or can be amended to provide), it may be possible to act under a provision similar to regulation 96 of Table A which allows the general meeting to waive the 'non-voting' regulation, either generally or in relation to a specified contract.

Board committees

Subject to the articles, the board may appoint committees and delegate to them such powers (within their own powers) as they think fit. They may also define the procedure (chairman, quorum, etc.) to be adopted by such committees, or they may leave such matters for the committee to decide. A board committee need not be limited to board members – persons not on the board can also be appointed and the committee may have power to co-opt additional members, but, in the case of a 'listed' company, The Stock Exchange requires that the company's articles provide that: (1) co-opted members shall be less than half of the total committee; and (2) no resolution of the committee shall be effective unless a majority of the members of the committee present when the decision is taken are directors.

CHAPTER 11

Minutes

After the meeting – whether board meeting or general meeting – it will be the duty of the secretary to prepare the minutes from notes made during the meeting and to ensure that all decisions are implemented.

Procedure

The basic procedure is as follows:

1. A first draft will be submitted to the chairman.
2. Subject to his approval, copies of the draft minutes will be sent to all directors.
3. Steps must be taken to implement the decisions recorded in the minutes.
4. Subject to any comments from the directors, a fair copy will be typed into the minute book.
5. At the next meeting the chairman will ask whether those present agree the minutes are a correct record. If so agreed, the chairman will sign and date the minutes at the end and sign or initial previous pages as explained later.

The purpose of a board meeting is to make decisions, including business decisions, which should usually be implemented without delay. Authority to implement the decisions lies in the minutes, which, under section 382(2) of the Act, are evidence of the proceedings of the meeting as soon as they are signed by the chairman. Clearly, then, the best procedure is to draft the minutes as quickly as possible, secure at least provisional approval from the chairman and then use them as the basis for communicating the decisions to those who have to implement them. An efficient secretary will thus aim to distribute copies of (or extracts from) the draft minutes within, say, 24 hours after the meeting.

Since at least two drafts will be required quickly with a final copy later, the case for word-processing equipment will be obvious. Clearly, too, such equipment must have adequate built-in safeguards to ensure confidentiality.

Guidance on drafting minutes is given later. The style for setting out minutes is largely a matter of taste, but a convenient layout will be found in Appendix J. Where the board includes a number of executive directors who will be responsible for implementation, it can be a useful reminder at the 'second draft' stage to add beneath each minute words such as 'Action: Mr A. B. Clark'. Suitable coding can ensure the word-processor skips the footnote on the minute-book copy. Alternatively it may provide quicker reference if a column at the right-hand edge of the second draft is headed 'Action by', with appropriate initials level with each minute.

Where action has to be taken by persons who do not (and often should not) receive copies of the full minutes, it will be the secretary's responsibility to ensure they are informed, often with a suitable extract from the minutes. Again the convenience of a word-processor will be obvious. The secretary should work through the minutes item by item to ensure that the necessary instructions are given on every point.

Later it will be the secretary's responsibility to check that action has been taken. Where a long-term programme or some special target date is indicated, a diary note may be appropriate. In other cases it may be sufficient to check against a copy of the minutes when the agenda for the next meeting is being prepared, ticking items known to be implemented, enquiring about others and adding to the new agenda (possibly under 'Matters arising', or as a manuscript note on the chairman's copy only) where action has not been taken or where the board may wish to give further consideration.

The importance of this follow-up cannot be underestimated, yet it can put the secretary in a delicate position in relation to the directors. If in difficulty, his resort must be to the chairman of the board. If it is the chairman who has defaulted in doing what he promised, the secretary is in a difficult position indeed – difficult, but not impossible. With care and tact, and with some knowledge of the personalities of the individuals concerned, the experienced secretary will usually find a way of resolving such problems.

While practice varies, a further copy of the minutes of the previous meeting is often circulated with the agenda and board papers for the next meeting, especially if amendments have been made.

Occasionally an error in the draft minutes will not be noticed until after they have been typed into the minute book ready for signature. In such a case it would be perfectly in order, at any time prior to signature, to make a neat and obvious alteration to the incorrect minute, which the chairman should sign (or initial) before signing the minutes as a whole. However, once the minutes in the minute book have been signed, they must not be altered. If an error is discovered after signature, or if the board wishes to change an earlier decision, an amending minute should be agreed at a later meeting. In such a case it would be prudent – and permissible – to make a marginal note against the earlier minute (e.g. 'See also minute 1432, 1-3-86').

It is obviously prudent to have the minutes signed by the chairman at the earliest opportunity. The minutes can be signed either by the chairman of *that* meeting or by the chairman of the next succeeding meeting. Thus the minutes of a general meeting would be signed by the chairman of the next *board* meeting; they should not be left until the next general meeting. While minutes are usually signed at a meeting, it may be necessary (and would be perfectly proper) for the chairman to sign the minutes without reference to the board or anyone else, as soon as they have been entered in the minute book.

Drafting minutes

Minutes should record:

1. The name of the company.
2. The type of meeting (board meeting, finance committee meeting, annual general meeting, etc.).
3. Date, time and place of the meeting.
4. Persons present or attending. Persons present are those entitled to vote; others, such as the secretary, auditors and solicitors, are attending. For board meetings it is usual to list the names of all present or attending and to indicate if they attend for part only (e.g. 'Mr A. B. Smith, minutes 570–573 only'). For general meetings it is usual to list names of directors and senior officials only and indicate, for example, 'and 35 other members'. In all cases it should of course be evident that a quorum was present.
5. An accurate record of all proceedings, including, in the case of a general meeting, the precise wording of every proposition (including every amendment) put before the meeting with a statement that it was carried or lost. General meeting minutes are usually worded 'It was resolved that . . .', but board minutes are less formal and usually commence 'It was agreed that . . .'.

Minutes must be factual. They record the facts, and the facts cannot be altered. In other matters the proceedings are under the control of the meeting and the secretary must do as the meeting decides, but minutes are an exception. The meeting cannot require the secretary to produce a false record. Similarly, if a director asks that his dissent be recorded, the secretary must record his dissent; the majority cannot rule otherwise.

Minutes must be unambiguous. Particular care is needed with words like 'should', 'may' and 'will'. A competent secretary will always watch for the unintended ambiguity, and if a sentence is capable of a second meaning he will see it and will reword his minutes (or correspondence) accordingly.

Minutes must be impartial. They must record the decisions taken – what is done or agreed – but avoid any comment, favourable or unfavourable, on those decisions. It would be permissible to include sufficient explanation for anyone not at the meeting to understand the business, but the discussion leading to a decision should not be recorded except to the extent that it is essential explanation. Minutes must be distinguished from a report of the proceedings, which could quite properly record what was said.

It is particularly important not to attempt to record reasons for decisions. Can all the reasons be known? One person may express very strongly his own reasons for supporting or opposing a resolution, but the voting may be carried by others who may have had quite different reasons which they left unsaid.

To report only some of the reasons can be misleading and, as one well-known company learned to its cost, even dangerous if the proceedings are ever called into question, e.g. before the courts or a government commission.

For general meetings, and especially with special or extraordinary resolutions needing a three-fourths majority, and also where a poll is taken, it is usual (but not strictly essential) to record the number of votes cast for and against. In other cases (arguably in all cases) it is sufficient to record that 'it was resolved' or that the resolution was 'carried', 'carried by the requisite majority', 'carried *nem. con.*' (*nemine contradicente*, no one voting against) or 'carried unanimously' (all voting for, no one abstaining). With board meetings, 'it was agreed' is sufficient, but any director who voted against is entitled to have his dissent recorded in the minutes.

Minute books

Section 382 of the Act, which requires every company to keep minutes of general and board meetings, also requires the minutes to be kept in a minute book. Under section 722 a loose-leaf book is acceptable provided adequate precautions are taken for guarding against falsification and for facilitating its discovery.

Under section 723 a computer record is also acceptable in place of a minute book provided the record is capable of being reproduced in legible form. Again, adequate precautions must be taken against fraud, and these will depend on the design of the hardware and software. Much progress has been made in recent years, but the advances in computer fraud leave doubt whether existing safeguards are adequate. While computers are undoubtedly excellent for producing minutes, it is probably wisest at present to use the computer as a convenient means of preparing a permanent typed record rather than relying on magnetic memory or other esoteric devices.

For a small private company (where, typically, the directors and the shareholders are the same persons) a single book will suffice for the minutes of both board and general meetings. Indeed, there is no reason why other records, such as the register of members and the register of directors, should not be kept in the same book. Keeping that book in a locked cabinet, except when taken into the personal custody of the secretary, would provide adequate precautions against falsification.

Board minutes are confidential and it would be quite improper for the secretary to disclose them to anyone other than a director without proper authority. Minutes of general meetings, in contrast, must, under section 383, be kept at the registered office and be open to inspection by any member without charge during business hours. Alternatively, a member may require a copy, for which the company may not charge more than 2½p per 100 words.

For a larger company, therefore, and particularly a p.l.c., there is a practical (though not a legal) necessity to keep board minutes and general minutes in separate books, lest a shareholder exercising his statutory right to inspect the minutes of general meetings should thereby gain unauthorised access to board minutes. It may also be necessary to take more elaborate precautions against falsification.

Precautions against fraud

Handwritten minutes in bound books have not completely disappeared. They clearly provide the best safeguard against falsification, especially if pages as well as minutes are consecutively numbered. Handwriting is laborious, but it is possible to marry the bound book to modern word-processing equipment by typing the minutes on to loose sheets slightly smaller than the pages of the book into which they can be pasted. Every sheet (not just the last for each meeting) should be signed by the chairman, who should arrange his signature to start on the pasted sheet and finish on the bound page.

More usually the minute book will be a loose-leaf binder, in which case safeguards should be built into the covers. The minimum for a p.l.c. should be a strong thong binder secured by screw winding (the handle for which should *not* be left in the cavity usually built into the cover), while more elaborate precautions are commercially available, such as an individual lever lock as a safeguard against anyone bringing his own screw winder.

As a precaution against fraudulent additions it would be prudent to conclude each meeting with words such as 'That concluded the business of the meeting' or 'The next meeting will be held on . . .'. This, coupled with a reference at the start of the next meeting to the date of the minutes signed, will preclude a fraudulent interpolation either in any blank space at the end of one set of minutes or on a separate sheet.

In all cases, minutes should be numbered consecutively. For preference the numbers should run consecutively through the minute book (i.e., if the minutes of the first meeting run from 1 to 17, then the minutes of the second meeting should start at 18) as a precaution, especially where a loose-leaf minute book is used, against fraudulent manipulation, whether by removal or interpolation.

Precautions should also be taken with the loose pages. Unused sheets should not be left within the binder but kept elsewhere under lock and key. Some companies have the company name printed on to each page with a serial sheet number, this being either at the top of each page or hidden within the binding margin. Some company secretaries initial each sheet as soon as the wording has been checked, usually again out of sight within the binding margin, while the chairman when he signs the minutes should also sign, or at least initial, every sheet used and not just the last page for each meeting.

Legal significance of minutes

Minutes, when signed by the chairman of that or the next succeeding meeting, are prima-facie evidence of the proceedings at the meeting, under section 382(2) of the Act.

Since they are only prima-facie evidence, they could be upset by other evidence to show they were erroneous, incomplete or even fraudulent, but any instance of this is hard to find. Until the contrary is shown, they can (if signed) be relied upon.

The signed minutes are thus the authority for the officers of the company to do whatever the meeting has decided.

Minutes are from time to time required as evidence, either in court proceedings or for routine matters such as evidence that a new director is duly appointed and has, for example, authority to sign cheques. In court proceedings it may be necessary to produce the actual minute book signed by the chairman (and for this reason it may occasionally be necessary for the chairman to sign without waiting for the authority of the next board meeting), but in most cases it will be sufficient to produce a typed extract from the minute book, this extract being certified correct by the signature of the secretary pursuant to section 41 of the Act.

The usual practice is to type the extract from the minutes on to a sheet of paper (preferably but not essentially the company's printed letter-paper) followed by such words as: 'Certified a true extract from the minutes of a meeting of the directors of .... p.l.c. held on [*date*]'. The secretary can then sign, usually having his name, the word 'Secretary' and the date he signs typed below his signature.

Occasionally an attempt is made to enforce a minute as if it were a contract. Minutes are not a contract, but may be evidence of a contract. This can be useful to the company or to an individual director, but anyone else may have difficulty in obtaining a copy unless in legal proceedings the court is prepared to issue a *subpoena duces tecum*, which is, in effect, an order to the secretary to bring the minute book into court. Faced with this prospect, most secretaries would doubtless prefer to ask permission from the board to offer an extract from minutes certified as above.

In any case, the possibility that this can happen may serve as a salutary reminder that care as well as speed is needed when drafting minutes.

Resolution in writing

Articles invariably include a provision similar to regulation 93 of Table A by which a resolution in writing signed by all the directors (or by all the directors entitled to notice, which may exclude directors overseas) is as effectual as if passed at a board meeting. Private company articles often include a provision on the lines of regulation 53 of Table A, offering a similar facility for members' resolutions.

This is obviously convenient if a single non-controversial resolution is required in an emergency or between regular meetings. For a small company it can replace a complete meeting. The usual practice is to type on a sheet of paper, preferably a sheet to fit the loose-leaf minute book, the heading 'Resolution in writing' and words such as: 'We being all the directors [*or* shareholders] of .... p.l.c. hereby resolve as follows . . .' The wording of the resolution will then be typed, below which each director will sign.

Every director (or every director entitled to notice) must sign, but it is not essential that every director signs the same sheet of paper. If separate sheets are used, the resolution must be identical, but the incidental wording could vary. In an emergency a director could be sent a telex: 'The chairman proposes the following. If you agree please sign your copy of this telex and post it back to me, cofirming by telex that you have done so.' Facsimile transmission could be used similarly, and in neither case is any variation required in the wording of the regulation in the articles. In all cases the resolution is effective as soon as all directors have signed; there is no need to wait until all copies are in the hands of the secretary, although care should obviously be taken.

If a director has some personal financial interest in the substance of the resolution and is thereby debarred from voting upon it, he must still sign if it is to be effective. This problem can be overcome by arranging that he signs at the foot beneath such words as: 'I sign for purposes of regulation 93 of the articles of association and not as a vote on the resolution.'

On completion the resolution should be given a serial number and the signed copy (or copies) secured into the minute book. It does not need to be signed again by the chairman at the next board meeting, but it would be a useful safeguard for the next minutes to record that the directors had noted that the resolution had been passed and entered in the minute book.

Private minutes

Board minutes are always confidential, but there are degrees of confidentiality. Every director is entitled to inspect the minute book and will usually receive a copy of the draft, which he will probably hand to his personal secretary to file. This may not matter greatly with routine board business but extra precautions may be prudent with certain details, such as salaries and other emoluments, or with 'price-sensitive' information, like a proposed share issue or plans to bid for another company. A simple and obvious precaution is to leave a blank at the appropriate point in the draft minutes, e.g.: '. . . at a salary of £   per annum'. The actual figure need appear in only one copy of the minutes – the final version in the minute book itself. Where such special confidentiality needs to be extended beyond matters of just a single name or a few figures – the detailed terms of a proposed take-over bid, for example – it may be better to refer to a separate document: '. . . on terms set out in a confidential memorandum from the Secretary, dated 1st December 1986 and initialled for identification by the Chairman'. The signed and initialled memorandum can then be pasted into the minute book, or at least kept under lock and key with the minutes.

Where such a situation occurs frequently it is good practice to keep a private minute book. This can be similar to the board minute book, but will frequently have a locking catch across the opening edges. Convenience would suggest that paper the same size as that of the board minutes be used, so that the same stock of loose-leaf pages can serve either purpose. However, where there is a need for greater security, often a smaller size should be used as a precaution against inserting sheets in the wrong binder.

The minutes recorded in the private minute book must of course be 'tied in' to the main minute book. In some cases the main minute book may record the full terms of a staff appointment or a salary increase, except for one or more figures which are left blank; the whole minute can then be repeated in the private minute book with the inclusion of the confidential figures. It may be preferable to record in the main minute book: 'at a salary and with other emoluments recorded in the private minute book'. If the whole subject is considered highly confidential it may be best to record in the main minute book: 'Minute 9876, Group Development (See private minute book)'. Private minutes are sometimes given their own consecutive serial numbers, tied in with such words as: '. . . as recorded in private minute 123', but it is usually better to give them the same serial numbers as the reference minutes in the main minute book. The fact that serial numbers in the private minute book will then not run consecutively presents neither practical difficulty nor security risk.

CHAPTER 12

Coping with disorder

The great majority of company meetings run smoothly. They may or may not be worthy show-places at which the company can demonstrate its competence and efficiency, but at least they do not dissolve into acrimony and disorder with the chairman wishing that, like Parliament, he had a serjeant-at-arms on hand to eject trouble-makers.

Just occasionally things are different. Debate becomes argument, with accusations and insults shouted across the room or even recourse to violence. What can then be done?

The first line of defence must of course be to try to avoid disorder. Much of this book has been written with that in mind. Not only must the meeting be planned with care, but it must be *seen* to be well planned: its conduct at every point must be such as to inspire confidence and the chairman must show a clear determination to conduct the meeting in a businesslike manner and to carry through all the items on the agenda.

Essential preliminaries are adequate seating, a prompt start and an experienced chairman. If trouble seems likely, a few stewards who could, if necessary, eject troublemakers would be useful. Their obvious presence could avoid the need for their services.

The chairman

The chairman needs to be experienced *as chairman*, i.e. in the conduct of meetings. He must be firm yet fair and tactful, he needs a sense of humour, but above all he must command the respect of the meeting. It has been known for a shareholder to criticise the board in strongest terms, but conclude by proposing a vote of thanks to the chairman for the way he has conducted the meeting. Such an accolade should be the aim of every chairman!

The prime duty of the chairman is to conduct the meeting to the point where all business has been completed. He may have discretion to deviate from the agenda, but he would be unwise to do so during a difficult meeting without good cause. While he must allow every opportunity for members to speak on relevant points, he should firmly resist speeches of undue length, or not concerned with the matter currently under discussion, or which merely repeat what has already been said.

Interruptions to raise points of order should be allowed, and if possible an immediate decision should be given. The occasional brief interjection should be tolerated. Otherwise, interruptions should be firmly discouraged – to the point where the persistent offender, after fair warning, should be asked to leave the meeting.

The chairman derives his powers from the articles, subject to which he must carry out the wishes of the meeting. For example, if adjournment is properly demanded and carried by an affirmative vote, the chairman must adjourn the meeting. Articles (e.g. regulation 45 of Table A) usually give him power to adjourn 'with the consent of the meeting', but he normally has no power to adjourn unless the meeting agrees. If, without such consent, he purports to adjourn and leaves, the meeting may elect another chairman and continue in his absence.

The chairman's duties in the course of debate, and particularly his duty to allow discussion and, on closing the discussion, to put the matter to the vote (if necessary, using his casting vote), have been covered in Chapters 5 and 6.

Expulsion

It is usual to admit to company meetings persons who have no legal entitlement to be there under the company's articles, such as the press, preference shareholders, legal advisers of members, or members of the company's staff. In most circumstances this is perfectly acceptable, provided all concerned recognise that they attend by invitation rather than by right and that they are not entitled to speak or vote or, indeed, to participate in any way in the business of the meeting. If necessary, the chairman can ask them to leave at any time and if they refuse to leave he can have them expelled from the meeting.

The expulsion of members is more difficult. A shareholder cannot be expelled from *membership* of the company in the way that a member of a social club can be expelled; while he holds shares he remains a member. Equally, if the articles give him the right to attend, he must be admitted to the meeting. However, if the meeting becomes so disorderly that business cannot reasonably be continued, the chairman may be faced with alternatives: either to adjourn the meeting in the hope that order may be restored when the meeting resumes or, if he can identify the trouble-maker, to eject him, member or not.

The power to eject should be used sparingly. It will lead to argument and may lead to legal action. If the need arises, the chairman should first ask the member concerned to resume his seat, i.e. to stop speaking. If he refuses, he should be reminded that the chairman has power to ask him to leave. When it becomes quite evident that he persistently refuses to accept the chairman's ruling, the chairman should ask him either to be quiet or to leave the room. The whole procedure should not be hurried. If the trouble-maker still persists, the chairman should approach him (being joined at this point by one or two stewards) and firmly ask him to sit down or leave. If all else fails, he may be ejected, with no more than reasonable force being used.

Experience shows that if sufficient firmness is shown in the early stages, provided time is taken and the procedure is not rushed, and particularly if it is made clear to the member that the chairman has power to expel and will reluctantly use that power if necessary, then the drama is unlikely to reach the final stages.

Needless to say, the secretary should record the proceedings with great care in the minutes, lest evidence be required in the event of legal action.

Free speech and defamation

It is sometimes overlooked that there are limits to the right of freedom of speech. Those limits may be exceeded by anything which is blasphemous, profane, seditious, abusive, defamatory or in contravention of the Official Secrets Act. While most of these can readily be avoided during a company meeting, the most likely offence is defamation.

Defamation is the publication of a statement which is injurious to a person's reputation or to his business occupation. Defamation may be slander if in transient form (e.g. spoken at a meeting) or libel if in permanent form (e.g. printed in the chairman's statement accompanying the accounts, or typed in a report of the meeting).

Slander will be actionable only if damage is proved or if the statement alleges a serious criminal offence, unfitness for office or for a trade or profession, or certain offences of a sexual character. Libel is always actionable. However, apart from the obvious defences of claiming the words are not in fact defamatory, or that they were not published (spoken, written, etc.) by the defendant, there are certain other defences:

1. *Justification.* Proof that the statement is true will be a complete defence, since the law will not allow a man to win damages with a reputation he ought not to have; but this is a defence to be used with care, since if it fails it will merely aggravate the defamation and augment the damages.
2. *Fair comment.* Comment on a matter of public interest (e.g. on the trading result of a 'listed' company, or on the way the chairman of such a company has conducted its annual general meeting) is allowed provided: (1) the comment is based on facts which can be proved to be true; (2) it is fair; and (3) it is truly a comment rather than an allegation of fact. The borderline between comment and an allegation of fact is sadly ill defined.
3. *Privilege.* If the person publishing the defamation had a public duty or a duty to the person to whom he communicated, then the occasion will be one of qualified privilege, offering a defence provided the communication was free of malice and did not go beyond the limits of that duty, e.g. by giving unnecessary additional information or by publication to a wider audience than circumstances required.
4. *Amends.* Defamation during or in relation to a meeting is rarely deliberate. The Defamation Act 1952 allows anyone who has published an innocent defamation to offer amends, i.e. to offer to publish a correction, with a suitable apology, to those to whom the original defamation was

published. If the offer is accepted, there can be no legal proceedings.

If it is not accepted, it will be sufficient to prove: (1) that the publisher did not intend to defame; (2) that the statement did not appear defamatory, the publisher did not know the special circumstances which made it so, and he exercised due care to avoid defamation; and (3) that the offer of amends was made as soon as practicable.

A sense of humour

A wise chairman will always seek to avoid conflict. In this he may well find a sense of humour, or even gentle irony, to be his most potent weapon.

This is such a personal matter, depending on the taste and skill of the individual, that it cannot be learned from a book; but perhaps two examples may provide food for thought and indicate how harmony can be restored.

Some years ago a shareholder criticised the chairman's statement because it described the company's products by obscure technical names. 'For example,' he said, 'what are surfactants? I am sure none of the shareholders knows!'

The chairman smiled, suggested most shareholders did know, and invited the shareholder sitting next to the questioner to explain. This shareholder gave a simple technical explanation, to the chagrin of the earlier speaker. It was not until after the meeting that the chairman explained the enquirer happened to be sitting next to the company's senior technical manager, who was also a shareholder.

The second example is taken from the annual general meeting of a company whose articles restricted attendance to those who had held at least 100 shares for at least one month. After one speaker had been criticising the company and the board fiercely for some time, the secretary noticed the registrar at the back of the hall waving frantically. Receiving a sign from the secretary to write, the registrar passed him a note to the effect that the speaker was a Mr X who held 100 shares but had possessed them only for two weeks. He was therefore not entitled to be present, let alone speak and vote. The secretary handed the note to the chairman and sat back to await the explosion.

The chairman read the note and rose to his feet, saying: 'I am sorry to interrupt, but I have just received a message. Is there a Mr X in the hall?' When the speaker, after a pause, admitted that was his name, the chairman asked: 'Are you the Mr X who only holds 100 shares and has only held them for two weeks?' Roars of laughter negated all criticism and the speaker realised he could not continue.

Humour and quick wit can turn an uncomfortable situation into a successful meeting.

CHAPTER 13

Personal preparation

Most of this book is concerned with physical preparations: the room, the facilities and the paperwork. But a meeting is a meeting of people. Everyone is different. Much will therefore depend upon the personal abilities of those, particularly the chairman and the secretary, who are in charge of proceedings. Knowing the subject is essential, but the ability to explain, to convince or to deal with unexpected opposition can be far more important.

To some the conduct of a meeting seems almost second nature so that no surprise can catch them off guard. Others (perhaps most of us when we start) may be highly competent in other duties but feel diffidence and hesitation when required to speak before a crowd of strangers.

Company secretaries are particularly vulnerable to such shortcomings. We work not in large partnerships but in ones and twos. Our training and professional qualification is exacting, but it aims at a written examination and recognises that most of us will be largely desk-bound in the early stages of our careers. At our first opportunity to attend, as secretary, a board or general meeting, we should know all the facts, but will we find ourselves tongue-tied?

This chapter aims to help those facing this problem.

Know your subject

It is a truism that qualification as a company secretary is the shortest route to the boardroom. It is an inevitable consequence that many secretaries arrive there as the most junior, least experienced person at the boardroom table.

It may seem elementary to suggest the secretary facing his first meeting should be sure he knows his subject, but it does require thought. Directors, even the chairman, are allowed (indeed, expected) to specialise. If the subject is sales, for example, neither the technical director nor the production director will be expected to contribute much, and similarly if the problem is any other speciality. But nearly every subject entails figures and personnel, while most require at least an outline knowledge of the law and many require some knowledge of finance or of tax. It is ironic that the secretary, often the least experienced person, is all too often expected to be able to contribute at least something on nearly everything.

The first advice to the new company secretary is therefore to know as much as possible of his subject, but also to know his limitations. Better to say he does not know, or that one of the specialist directors knows more, than to guess and risk error. Better still to offer to find out, perhaps to report to the next meeting.

Of course, this cannot apply to points of procedure concerning the meeting itself, especially at a shareholders' meeting. On that, the secretary *is* the expert.

It is sometimes said that the businessman does not think much of a lawyer unless he consults heavy volumes and takes time to consider, whereas he thinks little of the secretary who *does* need to consult books or who takes more than a few seconds to answer. Unfair, but all too true!

This does not mean the secretary should leave his books at home. As a minimum he should take to a general meeting the following:

1. The Companies Act 1985, with a good index.
2. Any subsequent legislation.
3. Memorandum and articles of association, with index. (The secretary may need to prepare his own index.)
4. This book, or a similar book on the practical conduct of meetings. Again, a good index for quick reference during the meeting is essential.

Finally, under this head, the secretary must study the agenda and ask himself what questions are likely to arise.

Some chairmen like to have, prior to a general meeting, a list of likely questions with prepared answers. However, experience shows that shareholders rarely ask the questions expected, so that it is better to try to forecast the *range* of subjects on which questions may be asked, and ensure the answers are in the room. For example, a great many questions could be asked on the published accounts; to forecast them could be self-defeating, and so it is better simply to make sure the chief accountant is in attendance with such details and supporting schedules as will enable him to provide a prompt and certain answer. Similarly for other specialities, depending on the agenda.

Be ready to speak

The best preparation, the fullest paperwork, is useless unless the secretary is ready and able to say what is necessary in a manner that is not just authoritative but also convincing. It is on this point that so many fail, with adverse consequences for their progress.

The remedy is not something that can be learned from a book. A few suggestions are made below, but ultimately you learn to speak only by speaking.

This may sound like a 'Catch 22' situation. If you do not know how to speak in public, how can you practise speaking in public? The answer is to start on a very modest scale. It is easier to ask a question than to answer one, and so practise asking first. Think up a question on the accounts. Write it out. Shorten it. Cut out all unnecessary words until less than ten are left. (If you cannot do that, it may be best to scrap the question and start again.) Then in the quietness of your own room ask the question aloud. Ask it again before a mirror. Ask it to a tape recorder and listen critically. When you feel confident, go to the annual general meeting of *some other company* where you are unknown, choose your moment and then spring to your feet and ask your question.

On such small beginnings a successful career can be built, but remember it is only a beginning. Go on to ask longer, more difficult questions. Attend meetings of the local branch of your professional institute (where you may not be unknown but where at least the audience will be sympathetic) and make a point of speaking at least once at each meeting. Before long you will find it easy.

Therein lies the next danger. Having overcome his initial shyness, a speaker is apt to talk too long. How long is too long? If there is one word that adds nothing to the message, then that speech is too long. Go back where you started, write out what you propose to say (do not dictate it – we are all verbose when we dictate) and cut out every superfluous word until you have a short, convincing speech. Use the tape recorder again, listen and ask yourself whether impact is lost in the length. The best advice that can be offered is: 'Stand up, speak up, then shut up!'

The real test of confidence is the ability to 'think on your feet', providing a ready answer when there is no opportunity for preparation. This, too, can come only with practice. The man of 60 may have learned this art in his youth at a debating society but, alas, such societies hardly exist today even in the better schools and universities. The remedy would appear to lie with tutors and the programmes of the branches of professional institutes.

A course of lectures on the law of meetings or the annual programme of the local branch of your institute could readily include a debate – or, better, a mock annual general meeting. A good tutor or branch chairman will try to ensure that everyone present speaks at least once.

One lecturer trying to organise a mock company meeting adopted the technique of shuffling and distributing small index cards, asking one student to question the accounts, another to challenge some point of procedure and yet another to propose a cut in the auditors' fees. By the end of term the cards would invite students without warning to make defamatory remarks about the chairman or the auditors – and by this time it was a student selected in rotation, not the lecturer, who was in the chair. Some of those sessions, considered as company meetings, were disastrous, but it is likely that most of the students learned something to develop their careers. At worst they made their mistakes in the privacy of a lecture room and not at a public meeting where a distraught chairman was trying to cope with disgruntled shareholders!

APPENDIX A

Articles of association

(Table A from the Companies (Tables A to F) Regulations 1985)

TABLE A

REGULATIONS FOR MANAGEMENT OF A COMPANY LIMITED BY SHARES

INTERPRETATION

1. In these regulations—

"the Act" means the Companies Act 1985 including any statutory modification or re-enactment thereof for the time being in force.

"the articles" means the articles of the company.

"clear days" in relation to the period of a notice means that period excluding the day when the notice is given or deemed to be given and the day for which it is given or on which it is to take effect.

"executed" includes any mode of execution.

"office" means the registered office of the company.

"the holder" in relation to shares means the member whose name is entered in the register of members as the holder of the shares.

"the seal" means the common seal of the company.

"secretary" means the secretary of the company or any other person appointed to perform the duties of the secretary of the company, including a joint, assistant or deputy secretary.

"the United Kingdom" means Great Britain and Northern Ireland.

Unless the context otherwise requires, words or expressions contained in these regulations bear the same meaning as in the Act but excluding any statutory modification thereof not in force when these regulations become binding on the company.

SHARE CAPITAL

2. Subject to the provisions of the Act and without prejudice to any rights attached to any existing shares, any share may be issued with such rights or restrictions as the company may by ordinary resolution determine.

3. Subject to the provisions of the Act, shares may be issued which are to be redeemed or are to be liable to be redeemed at the option of the company or the holder on such terms and in such manner as may be provided by the articles.

4. The company may exercise the powers of paying commissions conferred by the Act. Subject to the provision of the Act, any such commission may be satisfied by the payment of cash or by the allotment of fully or partly paid shares or partly in one way and partly in the other.

5. Except as required by law, no person shall be recognised by the company as holding any share upon any trust and (except as otherwise provided by the articles or by law) the company shall not be bound by or recognise any interest in any share except an absolute right to the entirety thereof in the holder.

SHARE CERTIFICATES

6. Every member, upon becoming the holder of any shares, shall be entitled without payment to one certificate for all the shares of each class held by him (and, upon transferring a part of his holding of shares of any class, to a certificate for the balance of such holding) or several certificates each for one or more of his shares upon payment for every certificate after the first of such reasonable sum as the directors may determine. Every certificate shall be sealed with the seal and shall specify the number, class and distinguishing numbers (if any) of the shares to which it relates and the amount or respective amounts paid up thereon. The company shall not be bound to issue more than one certificate for shares held jointly by several persons and delivery of a certificate to one joint holder shall be a sufficient delivery to all of them.

7. If a share certificate is defaced, worn-out, lost or destroyed, it may be renewed on such terms (if any) as to evidence and indemnity and payment of the expenses reasonably incurred by the company in investigating evidence as the directors may determine but otherwise free of charge, and (in the case of defacement or wearing-out) on delivery up of the old certificate.

LIEN

8. The company shall have a first and paramount lien on every share (not being a fully paid share) for all moneys (whether presently payable or not) payable at a fixed time or called in respect of that share. The directors may at any time declare any share to be wholly or in part exempt from the provisions of this regulation. The company's lien on a share shall extend to any amount payable in respect of it.

9. The company may sell in such manner as the directors determine any shares on which the company has a lien if a sum in respect of which the lien exists is presently payable and is not paid within fourteen clear days after notice has been given to the holder of the share or to the person entitled to it in consequence of the death or bankruptcy of the holder, demanding payment and stating that if the notice is not complied with the shares may be sold.

10. To give effect to a sale the directors may authorise some person to execute an instrument of transfer of the shares sold to, or in accordance with the directions of, the purchaser. The title of the transferee to the shares shall not be affected by any irregularity in or invalidity of the proceedings in reference to the sale.

11. The net proceeds of the sale, after payment of the costs, shall be applied in payment of so much of the sum for which the lien exists as is presently payable, and any residue shall (upon surrender to the company for cancellation of the certificate for the shares sold and subject to a like lien for any moneys not presently payable as existed upon the shares before the sale) be paid to the person entitled to the shares at the date of the sale.

CALLS ON SHARES AND FORFEITURE

12. Subject to the terms of allotment, the directors may make calls upon the members in respect of any moneys unpaid on their shares (whether in respect of nominal value or premium) and each member shall (subject to receiving at least fourteen clear days' notice specifying when and where payment is to be made) pay to the company as required by the notice the amount called on his shares. A call may be required to be paid by instalments. A call may, before receipt by the company of any sum due thereunder, be revoked in whole or part and payment of a call may be postponed in whole or part. A person upon whom a call is made shall remain liable for calls made upon him notwithstanding the subsequent transfer of the shares in respect whereof the call was made.

13. A call shall be deemed to have been made at the time when the resolution of the directors authorising the call was passed.

14. The joint holders of a share shall be jointly and severally liable to pay all calls in respect thereof.

15. If a call remains unpaid after it has become due and payable the person from whom it is due and payable shall pay interest on the amount unpaid from the day it became due and payable until it is paid at the rate fixed by the terms of allotment of the share or in the notice of the call or, if no rate is fixed, at the appropriate rate (as defined by the Act) but the directors may waive payment of the interest wholly or in part.

16. An amount payable in respect of a share on allotment or at any fixed date, whether in respect of nominal value or premium or as an instalment of a call, shall be deemed to be a call and if it is not paid the provisions of the articles shall apply as if that amount had become due and payable by virtue of a call.

17. Subject to the terms of allotment, the directors may make arrangements on the issue of shares for a difference between the holders in the amounts and times of payment of calls on their shares.

18. If a call remains unpaid after it has become due and payable the directors may give to the person from whom it is due not less than fourteen clear days' notice requiring payment of the amount unpaid together with any interest which may have accrued. The notice shall name the place where payment is to be made and shall state that if the notice is not complied with the shares in respect of which the call was made will be liable to be forfeited.

19. If the notice is not complied with any share in respect of which it was given may, before the payment required by the notice has been made, be forfeited by a resolution of the directors and the forfeiture shall include all dividends or other moneys payable in respect of the forfeited shares and not paid before the forfeiture.

20. Subject to the provisions of the Act, a forfeited share may be sold, re-alloted or otherwise disposed of on such terms and in such manner as the directors determine either to the person who was before the forfeiture the holder or to any other person and at any time before sale, re-allotment or other disposition, the forfeiture may be cancelled on such terms as the directors think fit. Where for the purposes of its disposal a forfeited share is to be transferred to any person the directors may authorise some person to execute an instrument of transfer of the share to that person.

21. A person any of whose shares have been forfeited shall cease to be a member in respect of them and shall surrender to the company for cancellation the certificate for the shares forfeited but shall remain liable to the company for all moneys which at the date of forfeiture were presently payable by him to the company in respect of those shares with interest at the rate at which interest was payable on those moneys before the forfeiture or, if no interest was so payable, at the appropriate rate (as defined in the Act) from the date of forfeiture until payment but the directors may waive payment wholly or in part or enforce payment without any allowance for the value of the shares at the time of forfeiture or for any consideration received on their disposal.

22. A statutory declaration by a director or the secretary that a share has been forfeited on a specified date shall be conclusive evidence of the facts stated in it as against all persons claiming to be entitled to the share and the declaration shall (subject to the execution of an instrument of transfer if necessary) constitute a good title to the share and the person to whom the share is disposed of shall not be bound to see to the application of the consideration, if any, nor shall his title to the share be affected by any irregularity in or invalidity of the proceedings in reference to the forfeiture or disposal of the share.

TRANSFER OF SHARES

23. The instrument of transfer of a share may be in any usual form or in any other form which the directors may approve and shall be executed by or on behalf of the transferor and, unless the share is fully paid, by or on behalf of the transferee.

24. The directors may refuse to register the transfer of a share which is not fully paid to a person of whom they do not approve and they may refuse to register the transfer of a share on which the company has a lien. They may also refuse to register a transfer unless—

(a) it is lodged at the office or at such other place as the directors may appoint and is accompanied by the certificate for the shares to which it relates and such other evidence as the directors may reasonably require to show the right of the transferor to make the transfer;

(b) it is in respect of only one class of shares; and

(c) it is in favour of not more than four transferees.

25. If the directors refuse to register a transfer of a share, they shall within two months after the date on which the transfer was lodged with the company send to the transferee notice of the refusal.

26. The registration of transfers of shares or of transfers of any class of shares may be suspended at such times and for such periods (not exceeding thirty days in any year) as the directors may determine.

27. No fee shall be charged for the registration of any instrument of transfer or other document relating to or affecting the title to any share.

28. The company shall be entitled to retain any instrument of transfer which is registered, but any instrument of transfer which the directors refuse to register shall be returned to the person lodging it when notice of the refusal is given.

TRANSMISSION OF SHARES

29. If a member dies the survivor or survivors where he was a joint holder, and his personal representatives where he was a sole holder or the only survivor of joint holders, shall be the only persons recognised by the company as having any title to his interest; but nothing herein contained shall release the estate of a deceased member from any liability in respect of any share which had been jointly held by him.

30. A person becoming entitled to a share in consequence of the death or bankruptcy of a member may, upon such evidence being produced as the directors may properly require, elect either to become the holder of the share or to have some person nominated by him registered as the transferee. If he elects to become the holder he shall give notice to the company to that effect. If he elects to have another person registered he shall execute an instrument of transfer of the share to that person. All the articles relating to the transfer of shares shall apply to the notice or instrument of transfer as if it were an instrument of transfer executed by the member and the death or bankruptcy of the member had not occurred.

31. A person becoming entitled to a share in consequence of the death or bankruptcy of a member shall have the rights to which he would be entitled if he were the holder of the share, except that he shall not, before being registered as the holder of the share, be entitled in respect of it to attend or vote at any meeting of the company or at any separate meeting of the holders of any class of shares in the company.

ALTERATION OF SHARE CAPITAL

32. The company may by ordinary resolution—

(a) increase its share capital by new shares of such amount as the resolution prescribes;

(b) consolidate and divide all or any of its share capital into shares of larger amount than its existing shares;

(c) subject to the provisions of the Act, sub-divide its shares, or any of them, into shares of smaller amount and the resolution may determine that, as between the shares resulting from the sub-division, any of them may have any preference or advantage as compared with the others; and

(d) cancel shares which, at the date of the passing of the resolution, have not been taken or agreed to be taken by any person and diminish the amount of its share capital by the amount of the shares so cancelled.

33. Whenever as a result of a consolidation of shares any members would become entitled to fractions of a share, the directors may, on behalf of those members, sell the shares representing the fractions for the best price reasonably obtainable to any person (including, subject to the provisions of the Act, the company) and distribute the net proceeds of sale in due proportion among those members, and the directors may authorise some person to execute an instrument of transfer of the shares to, or in accordance with the directions of, the purchaser. The transferee shall not be bound to see to the application of the purchase money nor shall his title to the shares be affected by any irregularity in or invalidity of the proceedings in reference to the sale.

34. Subject to the provisions of the Act, the company may by special resolution reduce its share capital, any capital redemption reserve and any share premium account in any way.

PURCHASE OF OWN SHARES

35. Subject to the provisions of the Act, the company may purchase its own shares (including any redeemable shares) and, if it is a private company, make a payment in respect of the redemption or purchase of its own shares otherwise than out of distributable profits of the company or the proceeds of a fresh issue of shares.

GENERAL MEETINGS

36. All general meetings other than annual general meetings shall be called extraordinary general meetings.

37. The directors may call general meetings and, on the requisition of members pursuant to the provisions of the Act, shall forthwith proceed to convene an extraordinary general meeting for a date not later than eight weeks after receipt of the requisition. If there are not within the United Kingdom sufficient directors to call a general meeting, any director or any member of the company may call a general meeting.

NOTICE OF GENERAL MEETINGS

38. An annual general meeting and an extraordinary general meeting called for the passing of a special resolution or a resolution appointing a person as a director shall be called by at least twenty-one clear days' notice. All other extraordinary general meetings shall be called by at least fourteen clear days' notice but a general meeting may be called by shorter notice if it is so agreed—

(*a*) in the case of an annual general meeting, by all the members entitled to attend and vote thereat; and

(*b*) in the case of any other meeting by a majority in number of the members having a right to attend and vote being a majority together holding not less than ninety-five per cent. in nominal value of the shares giving that right.

The notice shall specify the time and place of the meeting and the general nature of the business to be transacted and, in the case of an annual general meeting, shall specify the meeting as such.

Subject to the provisions of the articles and to any restrictions imposed on any shares, the notice shall be given to all the members, to all persons entitled to a share in consequence of the death or bankruptcy of a member and to the directors and auditors.

39. The accidental omission to give notice of a meeting to, or the non-receipt of notice of a meeting by, any person entitled to receive notice shall not invalidate the proceedings at that meeting.

PROCEEDINGS AT GENERAL MEETINGS

40. No business shall be transacted at any meeting unless a quorum is present. Two persons entitled to vote upon the business to be transacted, each being a member or a proxy for a member or a duly authorised representative of a corporation, shall be a quorum.

41. If such a quorum is not present within half an hour from the time appointed for the meeting, or if during a meeting such a quorum ceases to be present, the meeting shall stand adjourned to the same day in the next week at the same time and place or such time and place as the directors may determine.

42. The chairman, if any, of the board of directors or in his absence some other director nominated by the directors shall preside as chairman of the meeting, but if neither the chairman nor such other director (if any) be present within fifteen minutes after the time appointed for holding the meeting and willing to act, the directors present shall elect one of their number to be chairman and, if there is only one director present and willing to act, he shall be chairman.

43. If no director is willing to act as chairman, or if no director is present within fifteen minutes after the time appointed for holding the meeting, the members present and entitled to vote shall choose one of their number to be chairman.

44. A director shall, notwithstanding that he is not a member, be entitled to attend and speak at any general meeting and at any separate meeting of the holders of any class of shares in the company.

45. The chairman may, with the consent of a meeting at which a quorum is present (and shall if so directed by the meeting), adjourn the meeting from time to time and from place to place, but no business shall be transacted at an adjourned meeting other than business which might properly have been transacted at the meeting had the adjournment not taken place. When a meeting is adjourned for fourteen days or more, at least seven clear days' notice shall be given specifying the time and place of the adjourned meeting and the general nature of the business to be transacted. Otherwise it shall not be necessary to give any such notice.

46. A resolution put to the vote of a meeting shall be decided on a show of hands unless before, or on the declaration of the result of, the show of hands a poll is duly demanded. Subject to the provisions of the Act, a poll may be demanded—

(*a*) by the chairman; or

(*b*) by at least two members having the right to vote at the meeting; or

(*c*) by a member or members representing not less than one-tenth of the total voting rights of all the members having the right to vote at the meeting; or (*d*) by a member or members holding shares conferring a right to vote at the meeting being shares on which an aggregate sum has been paid up equal to not less than one-tenth of the total sum paid up on all the shares conferring that right;

and a demand by a person as proxy for a member shall be the same as a demand by the member.

47. Unless a poll is duly demanded a declaration by the chairman that a resolution has been carried or carried unanimously, or by a particular majority, or lost, or not carried by a particular majority and an entry to that effect in the minutes of the meeting shall be conclusive evidence of the fact without proof of the number or proportion of the votes recorded in favour of or against the resolution.

48. The demand for a poll may, before the poll is taken, be withdrawn but only with the consent of the chairman and a demand so withdrawn shall not be taken to have invalidated the result of a show of hands declared before the demand was made.

49. A poll shall be taken as the chairman directs and he may appoint scrutineers (who need not be members) and fix a time and place for declaring the result of the poll. The result of the poll shall be deemed to be the resolution of the meeting at which the poll was demanded.

50. In the case of an equality of votes, whether on a show of hands or on a poll, the chairman shall be entitled to a casting vote in addition to any other vote he may have.

51. A poll demanded on the election of a chairman or on a question of adjournment shall be taken forthwith. A poll demanded on any other question shall be taken either forthwith or at such time and place as the chairman directs not being more than thirty days after the poll is demanded. The demand for a poll shall not prevent the continuance of a meeting for the transaction of any business other than the question on which the poll was demanded. If a poll is demanded before the declaration of the result of a show of hands and the demand is duly withdrawn, the meeting shall continue as if the demand had not been made.

52. No notice need be given of a poll not taken forthwith if the time and place at which it is to be taken are announced at the meeting at which it is demanded. In any other case at least seven clear days' notice shall be given specifying the time and place at which the poll is to be taken.

53. A resolution in writing executed by or on behalf of each member who would have been entitled to vote upon it if it had been proposed at a general meeting at which he was present shall be as effectual as if it had been passed at a general meeting duly convened and held and may consist of several instruments in the like form each executed by or on behalf of one or more members.

VOTES OF MEMBERS

54. Subject to any rights or restrictions attached to any shares, on a show of hands every member who (being an individual) is present in person or (being a corporation) is present by a duly authorised representative, not being himself a member entitled to vote, shall have one vote and on a poll every member shall have one vote for every share of which he is the holder.

55. In the case of joint holders the vote of the senior who tenders a vote, whether in person or by proxy, shall be accepted to the exclusion of the votes of the other joint holders; and seniority shall be determined by the order in which the names of the holders stand in the register of members.

56. A member in respect of whom an order has been made by any court having jurisdiction (whether in the United Kingdom or elsewhere) in matters concerning mental disorder may vote, whether on a show of hands or on a poll, by his receiver, curator bonis or other person authorised in that behalf appointed by that court, and any such receiver, curator bonis or other person may, on a poll, vote by proxy.

Evidence to the satisfaction of the directors of the authority of the person claiming to exercise the right to vote shall be deposited at the office, or at such other place as is specified in accordance with the articles for the deposit of instruments of proxy, not less than 48 hours before the time appointed for holding the meeting or adjourned meeting at which the right to vote is to be exercised and in default the right to vote shall not be exercisable.

57. No member shall vote at any general meeting or at any separate meeting of the holders of any class of shares in the company, either in person or by proxy, in respect of any share held by him unless all moneys presently payable by him in respect of that share have been paid.

58. No objection shall be raised to the qualification of any voter except at the meeting or adjourned meeting at which the vote objected to is tendered, and every vote not disallowed at the meeting shall be valid. Any objection made in due time shall be referred to the chairman whose decision shall be final and conclusive.

59. On a poll votes may be given either personally or by proxy. A member may appoint more than one proxy to attend on the same occasion.

60. An instrument appointing a proxy shall be in writing, executed by or on behalf of the appointor and shall be in the following form (or in a form as near thereto as circumstances allow or in any other form which is usual or which the directors may approve)—

"

PLC/Limited

I/We, , of

, being a member/members of the above-named company, hereby appoint

of

, or failing him,

of , as my/our proxy to vote in my/our name[s] and on my/our behalf at the annual/extraordinary general meeting of the company to be held on 19 , and at any adjournment thereof.

Signed on 19 ."

61. Where it is desired to afford members an opportunity of instructing the proxy how he shall act the instrument appointing a proxy shall be in the following form (or in a form as near thereto as circumstances allow or in any other form which is usual or which the directors may approve)—

"

PLC/Limited

I/We, , of

, being a member/members of the above-named company, hereby appoint

of

, or failing him

of , as my/our proxy to vote in my/our name[s] and on my/our behalf at the annual/extraordinary general meeting of the company, to be held on 19 , and at any adjournment thereof.

This form is to be used in respect of the resolutions mentioned below as follows:

Resolution No. 1 *for *against
Resolution No. 2 *for *against.

*Strike out whichever is not desired.

Unless otherwise instructed, the proxy may vote as he thinks fit or abstain from voting.

Signed this day of 19 ."

62. The instrument appointing a proxy and any authority under which it is executed or a copy of such authority certified notarially or in some other way approved by the directors may—

(a) be deposited at the office or at such other place within the United Kingdom as is specified in the notice convening the meeting or in any instrument of proxy sent out by the company in relation to the meeting not less than 48 hours before the time for holding the meeting or adjourned meeting at which the person named in the instrument proposes to vote; or

(b) in the case of a poll taken more than 48 hours after it is demanded, be deposited as aforesaid after the poll has been demanded and not less than 24 hours before the time appointed for the taking of the poll; or

(c) where the poll is not taken forthwith but is taken not more than 48 hours after it was demanded, be delivered at the meeting at which the poll was demanded to the chairman or to the secretary or to any director;

and an instrument of proxy which is not deposited or delivered in a manner so permitted shall be invalid.

63. A vote given or poll demanded by proxy or by the duly authorised representative of a corporation shall be valid notwithstanding the previous determination of the authority of the person voting or demanding a poll unless notice of the determination was received by the company at the office or at such other place at which the instrument of proxy was duly deposited before the commencement of the meeting or adjourned meeting at which the vote is given or the poll demanded or (in the case of a poll taken otherwise than on the same day as the meeting or adjourned meeting) the time appointed for taking the poll.

NUMBER OF DIRECTORS

64. Unless otherwise determined by ordinary resolution, the number of directors (other than alternate directors) shall not be subject to any maximum but shall be not less than two.

ALTERNATE DIRECTORS

65. Any director (other than an alternate director) may appoint any other director, or any other person approved by resolution of the directors and willing to act, to be an alternate director and may remove from office an alternate director so appointed by him.

66. An alternate director shall be entitled to receive notice of all meetings of directors and of all meetings of committees of directors of which his appointor is a member, to attend and vote at any such meeting at which the director appointing him is not personally present, and generally to perform all the functions of his appointor as a director in his absence but shall not be entitled to receive any remuneration from the company for his services as an alternate director. But it shall not be necessary to give notice of such a meeting to an alternate director who is absent from the United Kingdom.

67. An alternate director shall cease to be an alternate director if his appointor ceases to be a director; but, if a director retires by rotation or otherwise but is reappointed or deemed to have been reappointed at the meeting at which he retires, any appointment of an alternate director made by him which was in force immediately prior to his retirement shall continue after his reappointment.

68. Any appointment or removal of an alternate director shall be by notice to the company signed by the director making or revoking the appointment or in any other manner approved by the directors.

69. Save as otherwise provided in the articles, an alternate director shall be deemed for all purposes to be a director and shall alone be responsible for his own acts and defaults and he shall not be deemed to be the agent of the director appointing him.

POWERS OF DIRECTORS

70. Subject to the provisions of the Act, the memorandum and the articles and to any directions given by special resolution, the business of the company shall be managed by the directors who may exercise all the powers of the company. No alteration of the memorandum or articles and no such direction shall invalidate any prior act of the directors which would have been valid if that alteration had not been made or that direction had not been given. The powers given by this regulation shall not be limited by any special power given to the directors by the articles and a meeting of directors at which a quorum is present may exercise all powers exercisable by the directors.

71. The directors may, by power of attorney or otherwise, appoint any person to be the agent of the company for such purposes and on such conditions as they determine, including authority for the agent to delegate all or any of his powers.

DELEGATION OF DIRECTORS' POWERS

72. The directors may delegate any of their powers to any committee consisting of one or more directors. They may also delegate to any managing director or any director holding any other executive office such of their powers as they consider desirable to be exercised by him. Any such delegation may be made subject to any conditions the directors may impose, and either collaterally with or to the exclusion of their own powers and may be revoked or altered. Subject to any such conditions, the proceedings of a committee with two or more members shall be governed by the articles regulating the proceedings of directors so far as they are capable of applying.

APPOINTMENT AND RETIREMENT OF DIRECTORS

73. At the first annual general meeting all the directors shall retire from office, and at every subsequent annual general meeting one-third of the directors who are subject to retirement by rotation or, if their number is not three or a multiple of three, the number nearest to one-third shall retire from office; but, if there is only one director who is subject to retirement by rotation, he shall retire.

74. Subject to the provisions of the Act, the directors to retire by rotation shall be those who have been longest in office since their last appointment or reappointment, but as between persons who became or were last reappointed directors on the same day those to retire shall (unless they otherwise agree among themselves) be determined by lot.

75. If the company, at the meeting at which a director retires by rotation, does not fill the vacancy the retiring director shall, if willing to act, be deemed to have been reappointed unless at the meeting it is resolved not to fill the vacancy or unless a resolution for the reappointment of the director is put to the meeting and lost.

76. No person other than a director retiring by rotation shall be appointed or reappointed a director at any general meeting unless—

(a) he is recommended by the directors; or

(b) not less than fourteen nor more than thirty-five clear days before the date appointed for the meeting, notice executed by a member qualified to vote at the meeting has been given to the company of the intention to propose that person for appointment or reappointment stating the particulars which would, if he were so appointed or reappointed, be required to be included in the company's register of directors together with notice executed by that person of his willingness to be appointed or reappointed.

77. Not less than seven nor more than twenty-eight clear days before the date appointed for holding a general meeting notice shall be given to all who are entitled to receive notice of the meeting of any person (other than a director retiring by rotation at the meeting) who is recommended by the directors for appointment or reappointment as a director at the meeting or in respect of whom notice has been duly given to the company of the intention to propose him at the meeting for appointment or reappointment as a director. The notice shall give the particulars of that person which would, if he were so appointed or reappointed, be required to be included in the company's register of directors.

78. Subject as aforesaid, the company may by ordinary resolution appoint a person who is willing to act to be a director either to fill a vacancy or as an additional director and may also determine the rotation in which any additional directors are to retire.

79. The directors may appoint a person who is willing to act to be a director, either to fill a vacancy or as an additional director, provided that the appointment does not cause the number of directors to exceed any number fixed by or in accordance with the articles as the maximum number of directors. A director so appointed shall hold office only until the next following annual general meeting and shall not be taken into account in determining the directors who are to retire by rotation at the meeting. If not reappointed at such annual general meeting, he shall vacate office at the conclusion thereof.

80. Subject as aforesaid, a director who retires at an annual general meeting may, if willing to act, be reappointed. If he is not reappointed, he shall retain office until the meeting appoints someone in his place, or if it does not do so, until the end of the meeting.

DISQUALIFICATION AND REMOVAL OF DIRECTORS

81. The office of a director shall be vacated if—

(*a*) he ceases to be a director by virtue of any provision of the Act or he becomes prohibited by law from being a director; or

(*b*) he becomes bankrupt or makes any arrangement or composition with his creditors generally; or

(*c*) he is, or may be, suffering from mental disorder and either—

(i) he is admitted to hospital in pursuance of an application for admission for treatment under the Mental Health Act 1983 or, in Scotland, an application for admission under the Mental Health (Scotland) Act 1960, or

(ii) an order is made by a court having jurisdiction (whether in the United Kingdom or elsewhere) in matters concerning mental disorder for his detention or for the appointment of a receiver, curator bonis or other person to exercise powers with respect to his property or affairs; or

(*d*) he resigns his office by notice to the company; or

(*e*) he shall for more than six consecutive months have been absent without permission of the directors from meetings of directors held during that period and the directors resolve that his office be vacated.

REMUNERATION OF DIRECTORS

82. The directors shall be entitled to such remuneration as the company may by ordinary resolution determine and, unless the resolution provides otherwise, the remuneration shall be deemed to accrue from day to day.

DIRECTORS' EXPENSES

83. The directors may be paid all travelling, hotel, and other expenses properly incurred by them in connection with their attendance at meetings of directors or committees of directors or general meetings or separate meetings of the holders of any class of shares or of debentures of the company or otherwise in connection with the discharge of their duties.

DIRECTORS' APPOINTMENTS AND INTERESTS

84. Subject to the provisions of the Act, the directors may appoint one or more of their number to the office of managing director or to any other executive office under the company and may enter into an agreement or arrangement with any director for his employment by the company or for the provision by him of any services outside the scope of the ordinary duties of a director. Any such appointment, agreement or arrangement may be made upon such terms as the directors determine and they may remunerate any such director for his services as they think fit. Any appointment of a director to an executive office shall terminate if he ceases to be a director but without prejudice to any claim to damages for breach of the contract of service between the director and the company. A managing director and a director holding any other executive office shall not be subject to retirement by rotation.

85. Subject to the provisions of the Act, and provided that he has disclosed to the directors the nature and extent of any material interest of his, a director notwithstanding his office—

(a) may be a party to, or otherwise interested in, any transaction or arrangement with the company or in which the company is otherwise interested;

(b) may be a director or other officer of, or employed by, or a party to any transaction or arrangement with, or otherwise interested in, any body corporate promoted by the company or in which the company is otherwise interested; and

(c) shall not, by reason of his office, be accountable to the company for any benefit which he derives from any such office or employment or from any such transaction or arrangement or from any interest in any such body corporate and no such transaction or arrangement shall be liable to be avoided on the ground of any such interest or benefit.

86. For the purposes of regulation 85—

(a) a general notice given to the directors that a director is to be regarded as having an interest of the nature and extent specified in the notice in any transaction or arrangement in which a specified person or class of persons is interested shall be deemed to be a disclosure that the director has an interest in any such transaction of the nature and extent so specified; and

(b) an interest of which a director has no knowledge and of which it is unreasonable to expect him to have knowledge shall not be treated as an interest of his.

DIRECTORS' GRATUITIES AND PENSIONS

87. The directors may provide benefits, whether by the payment of gratuities or pensions or by insurance or otherwise, for any director who has held but no longer holds any executive office or employment with the company or with any body corporate which is or has been a subsidiary of the company or a predecessor in business of the company or of any such subsidiary, and for any member of his family (including a spouse and a former spouse) or any person who is or was dependent on him, and may (as well before as after he ceases to hold such office or employment) contribute to any fund and pay premiums for the purchase or provision of any such benefit.

PROCEEDINGS OF DIRECTORS

88. Subject to the provisions of the articles, the directors may regulate their proceedings as they think fit. A director may, and the secretary at the request of a director shall, call a meeting of the directors. It shall not be necessary to give notice of a meeting to a director who is absent from the United Kingdom. Questions arising at a meeting shall be decided by a majority of votes. In the case of an equality of votes, the chairman shall have a second or casting vote. A director who is also an alternate director shall be entitled in the absence of his appointor to a separate vote on behalf of his appointor in addition to his own vote.

89. The quorum for the transaction of the business of the directors may be fixed by the directors and unless so fixed at any other number shall be two. A person who holds office only as an alternate director shall, if his appointor is not present, be counted in the quorum.

90. The continuing directors or a sole continuing director may act notwithstanding any vacancies in their number, but, if the number of directors is less than the number fixed as the quorum, the continuing directors or director may act only for the purpose of filling vacancies or of calling a general meeting.

91. The directors may appoint one of their number to be the chairman of the board of directors and may at any time remove him from that office. Unless he is unwilling to do so, the director so appointed shall preside at every meeting of directors at which he is present. But if there is no director holding that office, or if the director holding it is unwilling to preside or is not present within five minutes after the time appointed for the meeting, the directors present may appoint one of their number to be chairman of the meeting.

92. All acts done by a meeting of directors, or of a committee of directors, or by a person acting as a director shall, notwithstanding that it be afterwards discovered that there was a defect in the appointment of any director or that any of them were disqualified from holding office, or had vacated office, or were not entitled to vote, be as valid as if every such person had been duly appointed and was qualified and had continued to be a director and had been entitled to vote.

93. A resolution in writing signed by all the directors entitled to receive notice of a meeting of directors or of a committee of directors shall be as valid and effectual as if it had been passed at a meeting of directors or (as the case may be) a committee of directors duly convened and held and may consist of several documents in the like form each signed by one or more directors; but a resolution signed by an alternate director need not also be signed by his appointor and, if it is signed by a director who has appointed an alternate director, it need not be signed by the alternate director in that capacity.

94. Save as otherwise provided by the articles, a director shall not vote at a meeting of directors or of a committee of directors on any resolution concerning a matter in which he has, directly or indirectly, an interest or duty which is material and which conflicts or may conflict with the interests of the company unless his interest or duty arises only because the case falls within one or more of the following paragraphs—

(a) the resolution relates to the giving to him of a guarantee, security, or indemnity in respect of money lent to, or an obligation incurred by him for the benefit of, the company or any of its subsidiaries;

(b) the resolution relates to the giving to a third party of a guarantee, security, or indemnity in respect of an obligation of the company or any of its subsidiaries for which the director has assumed reponsibility in whole or part and whether alone or jointly with others under a guarantee or indemnity or by the giving of security;

(c) his interest arises by virtue of his subscribing or agreeing to subscribe for any shares, debentures or other securities of the company or any of its subsidiaries, or by virtue of his being, or intending to become, a participant in the underwriting or sub-underwriting of an offer of any such shares, debentures, or other securities by the company or any of its subsidiaries for subscription, purchase or exchange;

(d) the resolution relates in any way to a retirement benefits scheme which has been approved, or is conditional upon approval, by the Board of Inland Revenue for taxation purposes.

For the purposes of this regulation, an interest of a person who is, for any purpose of the Act (excluding any statutory modification thereof not in force when this regulation becomes binding on the company), connected with a director shall be treated as an interest of the director and, in relation to an alternate director, an interest of his appointor shall be treated as an interest of the alternate director without prejudice to any interest which the alternate director has otherwise.

95. A director shall not be counted in the quorum present at a meeting in relation to a resolution on which he is not entitled to vote.

96. The company may by ordinary resolution suspend or relax to any extent, either generally or in respect of any particular matter, any provision of the articles prohibiting a director from voting at a meeting of directors or of a committee of directors.

97. Where proposals are under consideration concerning the appointment of two or more directors to offices or employments with the company or any body corporate in which the company is interested the proposals may be divided and considered in relation to each director separately and (provided he is not for another reason precluded from voting) each of the directors concerned shall be entitled to vote and be counted in the quorum in respect of each resolution except that concerning his own appointment.

98. If a question arises at a meeting of directors or of a committee of directors as to the right of a director to vote, the question may, before the conclusion of the meeting, be referred to the chairman of the meeting and his ruling in relation to any director other than himself shall be final and conclusive.

SECRETARY

99. Subject to the provisions of the Act, the secretary shall be appointed by the directors for such term, at such remuneration and upon such conditions as they may think fit; and any secretary so appointed may be removed by them.

MINUTES

100. The directors shall cause minutes to be made in books kept for the purpose—

(a) of all appointments of officers made by the directors; and

(b) of all proceedings at meetings of the company, of the holders of any class of shares in the company, and of the directors, and of committees of directors, including the names of the directors present at each such meeting.

THE SEAL

101. The seal shall only be used by the authority of the directors or of a committee of directors authorised by the directors. The directors may determine who shall sign any instrument to which the seal is affixed and unless otherwise so determined it shall be signed by a director and by the secretary or by a second director.

DIVIDENDS

102. Subject to the provisions of the Act, the company may by ordinary resolution declare dividends in accordance with the respective rights of the members, but no dividend shall exceed the amount recommended by the directors.

103. Subject to the provisions of the Act, the directors may pay interim dividends if it appears to them that they are justified by the profits of the company available for distribution. If the share capital is divided into different classes, the directors may pay interim dividends on shares which confer deferred or non-preferred rights with regard to dividend as well as on shares which confer preferential rights with regard to dividend, but no interim dividend shall be paid on shares carrying deferred or non-preferred rights if, at the time of payment, any preferential dividend is in arrear. The directors may also pay at intervals settled by them any dividend payable at a fixed rate if it appears to them that the profits available for distribution justify the payment. Provided the directors act in good faith they shall not incur any liability to the holders of shares conferring preferred rights for any loss they may suffer by the lawful payment of an interim dividend on any shares having deferred or non-preferred rights.

104. Except as otherwise provided by the rights attached to shares, all dividends shall be declared and paid according to the amounts paid up on the shares on which the dividend is paid. All dividends shall be apportioned and paid proportionately to the amounts paid up on the shares during any portion or portions of the period in respect of which the dividend is paid; but, if any share is issued on terms providing that it shall rank for dividend as from a particular date, that share shall rank for dividend accordingly.

105. A general meeting declaring a dividend may, upon the recommendation of the directors, direct that it shall be satisfied wholly or partly by the distribution of assets and, where any difficulty arises in regard to the distribution, the directors may settle the same and in particular may issue fractional certificates and fix the value for distribution of any assets and may determine that cash shall be paid to any member upon the footing of the value so fixed in order to adjust the rights of members and may vest any assets in trustees.

106. Any dividend or other moneys payable in respect of a share may be paid by cheque sent by post to the registered address of the person entitled or, if two or more persons are the holders of the share or are jointly entitled to it by reason of the death or bankruptcy of the holder, to the registered address of that one of those persons who is first named in the register of members or to such person and to such address as the person or persons entitled may in writing direct. Every cheque shall be made payable to the order of the person or persons entitled or to such other person as the person or persons entitled may in writing direct and payment of the cheque shall be a good discharge to the company. Any joint holder or other person jointly entitled to a share as aforesaid may give receipts for any dividend or other moneys payable in respect of the share.

107. No dividend or other moneys payable in respect of a share shall bear interest against the company unless otherwise provided by the rights attached to the share.

108. Any dividend which has remained unclaimed for twelve years from the date when it became due for payment shall, if the directors so resolve, be forfeited and cease to remain owing by the company.

ACCOUNTS

109. No member shall (as such) have any right of inspecting any accounting records or other book or document of the company except as conferred by statute or authorised by the directors or by ordinary resolution of the company.

CAPITALISATION OF PROFITS

110. The directors may with the authority of an ordinary resolution of the company—

(a) subject as hereinafter provided, resolve to capitalise any undivided profits of the company not required for paying any preferential dividend (whether or not they are available for distribution) or any sum standing to the credit of the company's share premium account or capital redemption reserve;

(b) appropriate the sum resolved to be capitalised to the members who would have been entitled to it if it were distributed by way of dividend and in the same proportions and apply such sum on their behalf either in or towards paying up the amounts, if any, for the time being unpaid on any shares held by them respectively, or in paying up in full unissued shares or debentures of the company of a nominal amount equal to that sum, and allot the shares or

debentures credited as fully paid to those members, or as they may direct, in those proportions, or partly in one way and partly in the other: but the share premium account, the capital redemption reserve, and any profits which are not available for distribution may, for the purposes of this regulation, only be applied in paying up unissued shares to be allotted to members credited as fully paid;

(c) make such provision by the issue of fractional certificates or by payment in cash or otherwise as they determine in the case of shares or debentures becoming distributable under this regulation in fractions; and

(d) authorise any person to enter on behalf of all the members concerned into an agreement with the company providing for the allotment to them respectively, credited as fully paid, of any shares or debentures to which they are entitled upon such capitalisation, any agreement made under such authority being binding on all such members.

NOTICES

111. Any notice to be given to or by any person pursuant to the articles shall be in writing except that a notice calling a meeting of the directors need not be in writing.

112. The company may give any notice to a member either personally or by sending it by post in a prepaid envelope addressed to the member at his registered address or by leaving it at that address. In the case of joint holders of a share, all notices shall be given to the joint holder whose name stands first in the register of members in respect of the joint holding and notice so given shall be sufficient notice to all the joint holders. A member whose registered address is not within the United Kingdom and who gives to the company an address within the United Kingdom at which notices may be given to him shall be entitled to have notices given to him at that address, but otherwise no such member shall be entitled to receive any notice from the company.

113. A member present, either in person or by proxy, at any meeting of the company or of the holders of any class of shares in the company shall be deemed to have received notice of the meeting and, where requisite, of the purposes for which it was called.

114. Every person who becomes entitled to a share shall be bound by any notice in respect of that share which, before his name is entered in the register of members, has been duly given to a person from whom he derives his title.

115. Proof that an envelope containing a notice was properly addressed, prepaid and posted shall be conclusive evidence that the notice was given. A notice shall, unless the contrary is proved, be deemed to be given at the expiration of 48 hours after the envelope containing it was posted.

116. A notice may be given by the company to the persons entitled to a share in consequence of the death or bankruptcy of a member by sending or delivering it, in any manner authorised by the articles for the giving of notice to a member, addressed to them by name, or by the title of representatives of the deceased, or trustee of the bankrupt or by any like description at the address, if any, within the United Kingdom supplied for that purpose by the persons claiming to be so entitled. Until such an address has been supplied, a notice may be given in any manner in which it might have been given if the death or bankruptcy had not occurred.

WINDING UP

117. If the company is wound up, the liquidator may, with the sanction of an extraordinary resolution of the company and any other sanction required by the Act, divide among the members in specie the whole or any part of the assets of the company and may, for that purpose, value any assets and determine how the division shall be carried out as between the members or different classes of members. The liquidator may, with the like sanction, vest the whole or any part of the assets in trustees upon such trusts for the benefit of the members as he with the like sanction determines, but no member shall be compelled to accept any assets upon which there is a liability.

INDEMNITY

118. Subject to the provisions of the Act but without prejudice to any indemnity to which a director may otherwise be entitled, every director or other officer or auditor of the company shall be indemnified out of the assets of the company against any liability incurred by him in defending any proceedings, whether civil or criminal, in which judgment is given in his favour or in which he is acquitted or in connection with any application in which relief is granted to him by the court from liability for negligence, default, breach of duty or breach of trust in relation to the affairs of the company.

APPENDIX B

Statutory requirements

(Sections 366 to 383 from the Companies Act 1985)

Meetings and Resolutions

Meetings

Annual general meeting.

366.—(1) Every company shall in each year hold a general meeting as its annual general meeting in addition to any other meetings in that year, and shall specify the meeting as such in the notices calling it.

(2) However, so long as a company holds its first annual general meeting within 18 months of its incorporation, it need not hold it in the year of its incorporation or in the following year.

(3) Not more than 15 months shall elapse between the date of one annual general meeting of a company and that of the next.

(4) If default is made in holding a meeting in accordance with this section, the company and every officer of it who is in default is liable to a fine.

Secretary of State's power to call meeting in default.

367.—(1) If default is made in holding a meeting in accordance with section 366, the Secretary of State may, on the application of any member of the company, call, or direct the calling of, a general meeting of the company and give such ancillary or consequential directions as he thinks expedient, including directions modifying or supplementing, in relation to the calling, holding and conduct of the meeting, the operation of the company's articles.

(2) The directions that may be given under subsection (1) include a direction that one member of the company present in person or by proxy shall be deemed to constitute a meeting.

(3) If default is made in complying with directions of the Secretary of State under subsection (1), the company and every officer of it who is in default is liable to a fine.

(4) A general meeting held under this section shall, subject to any directions of the Secretary of State, be deemed to be an annual general meeting of the company; but, where a meeting so held is not held in the year in which the default in holding the company's annual general meeting occurred, the meeting so held shall not be treated as the annual general meeting for the year in which it is held unless at that meeting the company resolves that it be so treated.

(5) Where a company so resolves, a copy of the resolution shall, within 15 days after its passing, be forwarded to the registrar of companies and recorded by him; and if default is made in complying with this subsection, the company and every officer of it who is in default is liable to a fine and, for continued contravention, to a daily default fine.

368.—(1) The directors of a company shall, on a members' requisition, forthwith proceed duly to convene an extraordinary general meeting of the company. Extraordinary general meeting on members' requisition.

This applies notwithstanding anything in the company's articles.

(2) A members' requisition is a requisition of—

(*a*) members of the company holding at the date of the deposit of the requisition not less than one-tenth of such of the paid-up capital of the company as at that date carries the right of voting at general meetings of the company; or

(*b*) in the case of a company not having a share capital, members of it representing not less than one-tenth of the total voting rights of all the members having at the date of deposit of the requisition a right to vote at general meetings.

(3) The requisition must state the objects of the meeting, and must be signed by the requisitionists and deposited at the registered office of the company, and may consist of several documents in like form each signed by one or more requisitionists.

(4) If the directors do not within 21 days from the date of the deposit of the requisition proceed duly to convene a meeting, the requisitionists, or any of them representing more than one half of the total voting rights of all of them, may themselves convene a meeting, but any meeting so convened shall not be held after the expiration of 3 months from that date.

(5) A meeting convened under this section by requisitionists shall be convened in the same manner, as nearly as possible, as that in which meetings are to be convened by directors.

(6) Any reasonable expenses incurred by the requisionists by reason of the failure of the directors duly to convene a meeting shall be repaid to the requisitionists by the company, and any sum so repaid shall be retained by the company out of any sums due or to become due from the company by way of fees or other remuneration in respect of their services to such of the directors as were in default.

(7) In the case of a meeting at which a resolution is to be proposed as a special resolution, the directors are deemed not to have duly convened the meeting if they do not give the notice required for special resolutions by section 378(2).

Length of notice for calling meetings.

369.—(1) A provision of a company's articles is void in so far as it provides for the calling of a meeting of the company (other than an adjourned meeting) by a shorter notice than—

(*a*) in the case of the annual general meeting, 21 days' notice in writing; and

(*b*) in the case of a meeting other than an annual general meeting or a meeting for the passing of a special resolution—

(i) 7 days' notice in writing in the case of an unlimited company, and

(ii) otherwise, 14 days' notice in writing.

(2) Save in so far as the articles of a company make other provision in that behalf (not being a provision avoided by subsection (1)), a meeting of the company (other than an adjourned meeting) may be called—

(*a*) in the case of the annual general meeting, by 21 days' notice in writing; and

(*b*) in the case of a meeting other than an annual general meeting or a meeting for the passing of a special resolution—

(i) by 7 days' notice in writing in the case of an unlimited company, and

(ii) otherwise, 14 days' notice in writing.

(3) Notwithstanding that a meeting is called by shorter notice than that specified in subsection (2) or in the company's articles (as the case may be), it is deemed to have been duly called if it is so agreed—

(*a*) in the case of a meeting called as the annual general meeting, by all the members entitled to attend and vote at it; and

(*b*) otherwise, by the requisite majority.

(4) The requisite majority for this purpose is a majority in

number of the members having a right to attend and vote at the meeting, being a majority—

(*a*) together holding not less than 95 per cent. in nominal value of the shares giving a right to attend and vote at the meeting; or

(*b*) in the case of a company not having a share capital, together representing not less than 95 per cent. of the total voting rights at that meeting of all the members.

General provisions as to meetings and votes.

370.—(1) The following provisions have effect in so far as the articles of the company do not make other provision in that behalf.

(2) Notice of the meeting of a company shall be served on every member of it in the manner in which notices are required to be served by Table A (as for the time being in force).

(3) Two or more members holding not less than one-tenth of the issued share capital or, if the company does not have a share capital, not less than 5 per cent. in number of the members of the company may call a meeting.

(4) Two members personally present are a quorum.

(5) Any member elected by the members present at a meeting may be chairman of it.

(6) In the case of a company originally having a share capital, every member has one vote in respect of each share or each £10 of stock held by him; and in any other case every member has one vote.

Power of court to order meeting.

371.—(1) If for any reason it is impracticable to call a meeting of a company in any manner in which meetings of that company may be called, or to conduct the meeting in manner prescribed by the articles or this Act, the court may, either of its own motion or on the application—

(*a*) of any director of the company, or

(*b*) of any member of the company who would be entitled to vote at the meeting,

order a meeting to be called, held and conducted in any manner the court thinks fit.

(2) Where such an order is made, the court may give such ancillary or consequential directions as it thinks expedient; and these may include a direction that one member of the company present in person or by proxy be deemed to constitute a meeting.

(3) A meeting called, held and conducted in accordance with

an order under subsection (1) is deemed for all purposes a meeting of the company duly called, held and conducted.

Proxies.

372.—(1) Any member of a company entitled to attend and vote at a meeting of it is entitled to appoint another person (whether a member or not) as his proxy to attend and vote instead of him; and in the case of a private company a proxy appointed to attend and vote instead of a member has also the same right as the member to speak at the meeting.

(2) But, unless the articles otherwise provide—

(*a*) subsection (1) does not apply in the case of a company not having a share capital; and

(*b*) a member of a private company is not entitled to appoint more than one proxy to attend on the same occasion; and

(*c*) a proxy is not entitled to vote except on a poll.

(3) In the case of a company having a share capital, in every notice calling a meeting of the company there shall appear with reasonable prominence a statement that a member entitled to attend and vote is entitled to appoint a proxy or, where that is allowed, one or more proxies to attend and vote instead of him, and that a proxy need not also be a member.

(4) If default is made in complying with subsection (3) as respects any meeting, every officer of the company who is in default is liable to a fine.

(5) A provision contained in a company's articles is void in so far as it would have the effect of requiring the instrument appointing a proxy, or any other document necessary to show the validity of, or otherwise relating to, the appointment of a proxy, to be received by the company or any other person more than 48 hours before a meeting or adjourned meeting in order that the appointment may be effective.

(6) If for the purpose of any meeting of a company invitations to appoint as proxy a person or one of a number of persons specified in the invitations are issued at the company's expense to some only of the members entitled to be sent a notice of the meeting and to vote at it by proxy, then every officer of the company who knowingly and wilfully authorises or permits their issue in that manner is liable to a fine.

However, an officer is not so liable by reason only of the issue to a member at his request in writing of a form of appointment naming the proxy, or of a list of persons willing to act as proxy, if the form or list is available on request in writing to every member entitled to vote at the meeting by proxy.

(7) This section applies to meetings of any class of members of a company as it applies to general meetings of the company.

Right to demand a poll.

373.—(1) A provision contained in a company's articles is void in so far as it would have the effect either—

(*a*) of excluding the right to demand a poll at a general meeting on any question other than the election of the chairman of the meeting or the adjournment of the meeting ; or

(*b*) of making ineffective a demand for a poll on any such question which is made either—

(i) by not less than 5 members having the right to vote at the meeting ; or

(ii) by a member or members representing not less than one-tenth of the total voting rights of all the members having the right to vote at the meeting ; or

(iii) by a member or members holding shares in the company conferring a right to vote at the meeting, being shares on which an aggregate sum has been paid up equal to not less than one-tenth of the total sum paid up on all the shares conferring that right.

(2) The instrument appointing a proxy to vote at a meeting of a company is deemed also to confer authority to demand or join in demanding a poll ; and for the purposes of subsection (1) a demand by a person as proxy for a member is the same as a demand by the member.

Voting on a poll.

374. On a poll taken at a meeting of a company or a meeting of any class of members of a company, a member entitled to more than one vote need not, if he votes, use all his votes or cast all the votes he uses in the same way.

Representation of corporations at meetings.

375.—(1) A corporation, whether or not a company within the meaning of this Act, may—

(*a*) if it is a member of another corporation, being such a company, by resolution of its directors or other governing body authorise such person as it thinks fit to act as its representative at any meeting of the company or at any meeting of any class of members of the company;

(*b*) if it is a creditor (including a holder of debentures) of another corporation, being such a company, by resolution of its directors or other governing body authorise such person as it thinks fit to act as its representative at any meeting of creditors of the company held in pursuance of this Act or of rules made under it, or in pursuance of the provisions contained in any debenture or trust deed, as the case may be.

(2) A person so authorised is entitled to exercise the same powers on behalf of the corporation which he represents as that corporation could exercise if it were an individual shareholder, creditor or debenture-holder of the other company.

Resolutions

Circulation of members' resolutions.

376.—(1) Subject to the section next following, it is the duty of a company, on the requisition in writing of such number of members as is specified below and (unless the company otherwise resolves) at the expense of the requisitionists—

(*a*) to give to members of the company entitled to receive notice of the next annual general meeting notice of any resolution which may properly be moved and is intended to be moved at that meeting;

(*b*) to circulate to members entitled to have notice of any general meeting sent to them any statement of not more than 1,000 words with respect to the matter referred to in any proposed resolution or the business to be dealt with at that meeting.

(2) The number of members necessary for a requisition under subsection (1) is—

(*a*) any number representing not less than one-twentieth of the total voting rights of all the members having at the date of the requisition a right to vote at the meeting to which the requisition relates; or

(*b*) not less than 100 members holding shares in the company on which there has been paid up an average sum, per member, of not less than £100.

(3) Notice of any such resolution shall be given, and any such statement shall be circulated, to members of the company entitled to have notice of the meeting sent to them, by serving a copy of the resolution or statement on each such member in any manner permitted for service of notice of the meeting.

(4) Notice of any such resolution shall be given to any other member of the company by giving notice of the general effect of the resolution in any manner permitted for giving him notice of meetings of the company.

(5) For compliance with subsections (3) and (4), the copy must be served, or notice of the effect of the resolution be given (as the case may be), in the same manner and (so far as practicable) at the same time as notice of the meeting; and, where it is not practicable for it to be served or given at the same time, it must be served or given as soon as practicable thereafter.

(6) The business which may be dealt with at an annual general meeting includes any resolution of which notice is given in accordance with this section ; and for purposes of this subsection notice is deemed to have been so given notwithstanding the accidental omission, in giving it, of one or more members. This has effect notwithstanding anything in the company's articles.

(7) In the event of default in complying with this section, every officer of the company who is in default is liable to a fine.

In certain cases, compliance with s. 376 not required.

377.—(1) A company is not bound under section 376 to give notice of a resolution or to circulate a statement unless—

(*a*) a copy of the requisition signed by the requisitionists (or two or more copies which between them contain the signatures of all the requisitionists) is deposited at the registered office of the company—

(i) in the case of a requisition requiring notice of a resolution, not less than 6 weeks before the meeting, and

(ii) otherwise, not less than one week before the meeting; and

(*b*) there is deposited or tendered with the requisition a sum reasonably sufficient to meet the company's expenses in giving effect to it.

(2) But if, after a copy of a requisition requiring notice of a resolution has been deposited at the company's registered office, an annual general meeting is called for a date 6 weeks or less after the copy has been deposited, the copy (though not deposited within the time required by subsection (1)) is deemed properly deposited for the purposes of that subsection.

(3) The company is also not bound under section 376 to circulate a statement if, on the application either of the company or of any other person who claims to be aggrieved, the court is satisfied that the rights conferred by that section are being abused to secure needless publicity for defamatory matter; and

the court may order the company's costs on such an application to be paid in whole or in part by the requisitionists, notwithstanding that they are not parties to the application.

Extraordinary and special resolutions.

378.—(1) A resolution is an extraordinary resolution when it has been passed by a majority of not less than three-fourths of such members as (being entitled to do so) vote in person or, where proxies are allowed, by proxy, at a general meeting of which notice specifying the intention to propose the resolution as an extraordinary resolution has been duly given.

(2) A resolution is a special resolution when it has been passed by such a majority as is required for the passing of an extraordinary resolution and at a general meeting of which not less than 21 days' notice, specifying the intention to propose the resolution as a special resolution, has been duly given.

(3) If it is so agreed by a majority in number of the members having the right to attend and vote at such a meeting, being a majority—

(*a*) together holding not less than 95 per cent. in nominal value of the shares giving that right; or

(*b*) in the case of a company not having a share capital, together representing not less than 95 per cent. of the total voting rights at that meeting of all the members,

a resolution may be proposed and passed as a special resolution at a meeting of which less than 21 days' notice has been given.

(4) At any meeting at which an extraordinary resolution or a special resolution is submitted to be passed, a declaration by the chairman that the resolution is carried is, unless a poll is demanded, conclusive evidence of the fact without proof of the number or proportion of the votes recorded in favour of or against the resolution.

(5) In computing the majority on a poll demanded on the question that an extraordinary resolution or a special resolution be passed, reference is to be had to the number of votes cast for and against the resolution.

(6) For purposes of this section, notice of a meeting is deemed duly given, and the meeting duly held, when the notice is given and the meeting held in the manner provided by this Act or the company's articles.

Resolution requiring special notice.

379.—(1) Where by any provision of this Act special notice is required of a resolution, the resolution is not effective unless notice of the intention to move it has been given to the company at least 28 days before the meeting at which it is moved.

(2) The company shall give its members notice of any such

resolution at the same time and in the same manner as it gives notice of the meeting or, if that is not practicable, shall give them notice either by advertisement in a newspaper having an appropriate circulation or in any other mode allowed by the company's articles, at least 21 days before the meeting.

(3) If, after notice of the intention to move such a resolution has been given to the company, a meeting is called for a date 28 days or less after the notice has been given, the notice is deemed properly given, though not given within the time required.

380.—(1) A copy of every resolution or agreement to which this section applies shall, within 15 days after it is passed or made, be forwarded to the registrar of companies and recorded by him; and it must be either a printed copy or else a copy in some other form approved by the registrar.

Registration, etc. of resolutions and agreements.

(2) Where articles have been registered, a copy of every such resolution or agreement for the time being in force shall be embodied in or annexed to every copy of the articles issued after the passing of the resolution or the making of the agreement.

(3) Where articles have not been registered, a printed copy of every such resolution or agreement shall be forwarded to any member at his request on payment of 5 pence or such less sum as the company may direct.

(4) This section applies to—

(*a*) special resolutions;

(*b*) extraordinary resolutions;

(*c*) resolutions or agreements which have been agreed to by all the members of a company but which, if not so agreed to, would not have been effective for their purpose unless (as the case may be) they had been passed as special resolutions or as extraordinary resolutions;

(*d*) resolutions or agreements which have been agreed to by all the members of some class of shareholders but which, if not so agreed to, would not have been effective for their purpose unless they had been passed by some particular majority or otherwise in some particular manner, and all resolutions or agreements which effectively bind all the members of any class of shareholders though not agreed to by all those members;

(*e*) a resolution passed by the directors of a company in compliance with a direction under section 31(2) (change of name on Secretary of State's direction);

(*f*) a resolution of a company to give, vary, revoke or renew an authority to the directors for the purposes of section 80 (allotment of relevant securities);

(*g*) a resolution of the directors passed under section 147(2) (alteration of memorandum on company ceasing to be a public company, following acquisition of its own shares);

(*h*) a resolution conferring, varying, revoking or renewing authority under section 166 (market purchase of company's own shares);

(*j*) a resolution for voluntary winding up, passed under section 572(1)(*a*);

(*k*) a resolution passed by the directors of an old public company, under section 2(1) of the Consequential Provisions Act, that the company should be re-registered as a public company.

(5) If a company fails to comply with subsection (1), the company and every officer of it who is in default is liable to a fine and, for continued contravention, to a daily default fine.

(6) If a company fails to comply with subsection (2) or (3), the company and every officer of it who is in default is liable to a fine.

(7) For purposes of subsections (5) and (6), a liquidator of a company is deemed an officer of it.

Resolution passed at adjourned meeting.

381. Where a resolution is passed at an adjourned meeting of—

(*a*) a company;

(*b*) the holders of any class of shares in a company;

(*c*) the directors of a company;

the resolution is for all purposes to be treated as having been passed on the date on which it was in fact passed, and is not to be deemed passed on any earlier date.

Records of proceedings

Minutes of meetings.

382.—(1) Every company shall cause minutes of all proceedings of general meetings, all proceedings at meetings of its directors and, where there are managers, all proceedings at meetings of its managers to be entered in books kept for that purpose.

(2) Any such minute, if purporting to be signed by the chairman of the meeting at which the proceedings were had, or by the chairman of the next succeeding meeting, is evidence of the proceedings.

(3) Where a shadow director by means of a notice required by section 317(8) declares an interest in a contract or proposed contract, this section applies—

(*a*) if it is a specific notice under paragraph (*a*) of that subsection, as if the declaration had been made at the meeting there referred to, and

(*b*) otherwise, as if it had been made at the meeting of the directors next following the giving of the notice;

and the making of the declaration is in either case deemed to form part of the proceedings at the meeting.

(4) Where minutes have been made in accordance with this section of the proceedings at any general meeting of the company or meeting of directors or managers, then, until the contrary is proved, the meeting is deemed duly held and convened, and all proceedings had at the meeting to have been duly had; and all appointments of directors, managers or liquidators are deemed valid.

(5) If a company fails to comply with subsection (1), the company and every officer of it who is in default is liable to a fine and, for continued contravention, to a daily default fine.

383.—(1) The books containing the minutes of proceedings of any general meeting of a company held on or after 1st November 1929 shall be kept at the company's registered office, and shall during business hours be open to the inspection of any member without charge.

Inspection of minute books.

(2) The reference to business hours is subject to such reasonable restrictions as the company may by its articles or in general meeting impose, but so that not less than 2 hours in each day be allowed for inspection.

(3) Any member shall be entitled to be furnished, within 7 days after he has made a request in that behalf to the company, with a copy of any such minutes as are referred to above, at a charge of not more than 2½ pence for every 100 words.

(4) If an inspection required under this section is refused or if a copy required under this section is not sent within the proper time, the company and every officer of it who is in default is liable in respect of each offence to a fine.

(5) In the case of any such refusal or default, the court may by order compel an immediate inspection of the books in respect of all proceedings of general meetings, or direct that the copies required be sent to the persons requiring them.

APPENDIX C

Quick reference chart for notices, accounts, attendance and voting

	Entitled to			
	Notice	Accounts	Attend	Vote
Members: Voting shares	Yes	Yes	Yes	Yes
Non-voting shares	C	Yes	A	No
Preference shares	C	Yes	A	A
Members overseas (no UK address)	B	Yes	Yes	Yes
Personal reps of deceased members	C	Yes	B	B
Personal reps of bankrupt members	C	Yes	B	B
Receiver in mental disorder	A	A	C	C
Second (or later) holder on joint a/c	No	No	Yes	No
Members with calls unpaid	Yes	Yes	B	B
Debenture holders	No	Yes	No	No
Auditors	Yes	Yes	Yes	No

Notes: A Depends on articles or terms of issue
B Depends on articles: 'No' under Table A
C Depends on articles: 'Yes' under Table A

APPENDIX D

Timetable and checklist: AGM of a 'listed' company

(from audit to annual return)

	Target date
1. Audit completed	
2. Fix date of board meeting	
2.1. Notify Stock Exchange	
2.2. Notice of board meeting	
2.3. Invite auditors?	
2.4. Notify directors of date 'closed season' commences	
3. Board meeting held	
At conclusion:	
3.1. Two directors sign balance sheet(s)	
3.2. Secretary signs directors' report	
3.3. Auditors sign auditors' report	
3.4. Preliminary announcement to Stock Exchange	
4. Reports and accounts to printers	
5. Instruct registrar to:	
5.1. Send addressed envelopes (or labels) to printers	
5.2. Arrange to pay dividend	
6. Printers despatch reports, accounts, proxies	(M – 25)
7. Date notice deemed given (depends on articles)	(M – 23)
8. First clear day	(M – 22)
9. Registrars receive proxies	
10. Cut-off day (and time)	(M – 2)
11. 21st clear day	(M – 1)
12. Annual general meeting	(M Day)
At conclusion release dividend warrants	
13. File resolutions	(M + 14)
14. Record date for annual return	(M + 14)
15. Last day for filing annual return	(M + 42)
16. Make diary notes for next year	
17. Destroy proxy forms	

APPENDIX E

Checklist: selecting the room

Requirements will depend on numbers expected and likely length of meeting, but, as many rooms offered commercially are patently unsuitable, the following points merit checking before confirming a booking:

Ready access from street
- Public transport
- Adequate car parking
- If possible, access for disabled persons
- Provision for hats and coats
- Toilet facilities (both sexes)

Size of room in relation to attendance expected
- Overflow room?

Director's retiring room, if required (e.g. during adjournment)

Equipment
- Sufficient chairs
- Table (on dais?) for directors
- Table at entrance for attendance sheets
- Side table for press?
- Audio-amplification (*must* be tested)

Lighting

Acoustics
- Listen for traffic, office machinery, church bells, rival meetings in nearby rooms
- The chairman's voice must be audible in all parts of the room, above the rustle of papers

Ventilation

Telephone (coins or credit card required?)

Practicability of controlling gatecrashers and demonstrators if necessary

Catering facilities, if required

APPENDIX F

Checklist: what to take to the meeting

Requirements will depend on the expected size of the meeting and the nature of the business, but even in the worst eventualities the following should suffice:

Companies Act 1985, with index

Memorandum and articles of association – several copies, at least one with index

Report and accounts – plenty of copies

Chairman's extended agenda
  Notes on quorum, voting, proxies and polls
  Summary of proxies received

Documents for signature (e.g. copy of new articles to be 'signed by the chairman for purposes of identification')

Draft resolution typed on card (for shareholder re auditors, etc.)
  Matching card to pass shareholder's name to chairman

Notepads and pencils or ball-point pens

Direction signs (to help members find room)

Attendance sheets, ready for signature
  1. Members, proxies, corporate representatives
  2. Press
  3. Bankers, stockbrokers, others

Seat reservation cards, e.g.
  RESERVED SEAT
  CHAIRMAN
  SECRETARY
  AUDITORS
  PRESS
  VOTING SHAREHOLDERS ONLY THIS SIDE
  etc.

(Continued)

Voting slips, for use if poll demanded
    Original proxy forms
    Summary sheet(s) for use by scruntineers

Copy of register of members (or dividend list), if practicable

Coins (or credit card) for public telephone

APPENDIX G

Specimen notice for an AGM

EXAMPLE COMPANY p.l.c.

To the (ordinary) shareholders

NOTICE OF MEETING

The Annual General Meeting of Example Company p.l.c. will be held at [*place*] on [*date*] at [*time*] for the following purposes:

1. To consider the accounts for the year ended [*date*] and the reports thereon by the directors and the auditors.
2. To declare a dividend.
3. To re-elect directors.
4. To reappoint the auditors and (to authorise the directors) to fix their remuneration.
5. To consider and if thought fit pass the following resolution which will be proposed as a Special Resolution:

SPECIAL RESOLUTION

That the directors be and are hereby empowered, pursuant to the Companies Act 1985, section 95(1), to allot equity securities (as defined in section 94(2) of that Act) up to an aggregate nominal value of £1,000,000, this power to expire on the date of the next annual general meeting of the Company.

By order of the board,
I. Scribe,
Secretary

Registered office:
99 High Street,
Newtown,
Essex SS2 3ZZ
1st September 1986

(*Continued*)

Notes

1. A member entitled to attend and vote at this meeting may appoint one or more proxies to attend and, upon a poll, to vote for him. A proxy need not also be a member.
2. The register of directors' interests in the Company's securities and copies of all contracts under which directors of the Company are employed by the Company will be open for inspection at the registered office during normal business hours from the date of this notice until the day of the meeting and will be available at the meeting.

   Or:

   The register of directors' interests in the Company's securities will be open for inspection at the registered office during normal business hours from the date of this notice until the day of the meeting and will be available at the meeting. There are no contracts of service whereunder directors are employed by the Company other than contracts determinable by the Company within one year without compensation.

APPENDIX H

Chairman's notes or extended agenda

(based on the notice in Appendix G)

EXAMPLE COMPANY p.l.c.

To: The Chairman
From: The Secretary

NOTES FOR AGM, 1986

1. Notes on voting procedure (including proxies, demanding a poll and taking a poll) are attached.
2. Check amplifier working.
3. Promptly at [*time*] ask stewards to close door.
4. Check quorum. Three members are required; you and I plus either Mr White or Mr Green will suffice.
5. Welcome members.

Report and Accounts

6. Ask Mr Brown to propose:
   'That the report and accounts of the Company for the year to 30th June 1986 be received.'
7. Ask Mr White to second.
8. Ask Secretary to read the auditors' report.
   NB: The auditors' report must not be 'taken as read'.
9. Invite questions or discussion. Mr Grey (Secretary), Mr Tott (Chief Accountant) or Mr Stone (Auditor) will be available to answer.
   Avoid new information. If new information of a price-sensitive character is given at the meeting, it will be necessary to notify The Stock Exchange immediately and circularise all shareholders as quickly as possible.
10. After reasonable discussion ask members to vote and declare result. If voting is equal, use casting vote and declare carried. If motion defeated, demand a poll.

[Continue with appropriate headings and repeat paras. 6, 7, 9 and 10 (renumbered) for remaining ordinary resolutions.]

(*Continued*)

Share Pre-emption

30. Propose from the chair *as a special resolution*:
'That the directors be and are hereby empowered, pursuant to the Companies Act 1985, section 95(1), to allot equity securities (as defined in section 94(2) of that Act) up to an aggregate nominal value of £1,000,000, this power to expire on the date of the next annual general meeting of the Company.'
31. Invite questions or discussion. After reasonable discussion *remind members that a three-fourths majority is required* and ask them to vote. Declare result. (On a special resolution you do not have a casting vote.) If votes 'for' are not at least three times votes 'against', demand a poll.
32. Ask whether there is any other business. Only purely formal matters (such as questions, or a vote of thanks) should be accepted. Reject others on grounds that notice has not been given.
33. Formally close meeting, but invite members to join board for light refreshments. (They should turn right on leaving meeting-room. Notices indicate where refreshments are served.)

[Attached to these notes would be: (1) notes on voting procedure, including procedure for demanding and taking a poll, and (2) summary of proxies received, indicating votes 'for' and 'against' each resolution.]

APPENDIX J

Draft minutes of an AGM

(based on the notice in Appendix G)

EXAMPLE COMPANY p.l.c.

MINUTES

of the Annual General Meeting of the Company
held at [*place*] on [*date*] at [*time*]

Present:	Mr A. B. Black, Chairman	
	Mr C. D. Brown	Directors
	Mrs E. F. Green	Directors
	Miss G. H. Pink	Directors
	Mr J. K. Rose	Directors
	Mr L. M. White	Directors
	and 37 other members of the Company	
Attending:	Mr N. O. Grey, Secretary	
	Mr Stone of Stone & Co., Auditors	
	Mr Jones of David & Jones, Solicitors	
	Stockbrokers, representatives of the press and others	

1. Report and Accounts

There were laid before the meeting the Company's balance sheet and consolidated balance sheet at 30th June 1986, the consolidated profit and loss account for the accounting period ended on that date and the directors' and auditors' reports thereon. The Secretary read the auditors' report and the Chairman invited questions.

After a short discussion it was Resolved that the report and accounts of the Company for the year to 30th June 1986 be received.

2. Dividend

It was Resolved that a (final) dividend of .... pence per share be paid on [*date*] on the (ordinary) shares of the Company for the year ended [*date*] to shareholders registered at the close of business on [*date*].

3. Directors

It was Resolved that Mr A. B. Black, who is retiring in rotation, be and is hereby re-elected a director of the Company.

It was Resolved that Mrs E. F. Green, who is retiring in rotation, be and is hereby re-elected a director of the Company.

It was Resolved that Mr L. M. White, who is retiring, having been appointed a director since the last annual general meeting, be and is hereby re-elected a director of the Company.

4. Auditors

It was proposed by Mr R. S. Smith, an ordinary shareholder, seconded by Miss T. V. Robinson representing Investment Trust Limited, ordinary shareholders, and Resolved that Stone & Co., Chartered Accountants, be paid a fee of £......... [*or* a fee to be fixed by the directors] for the audit of the accounts for the period to 30th June 1986.

It was further Resolved that Stone & Co. be and are hereby reappointed auditors of the Company to hold office until the conclusion of the general meeting at which the Company's next annual accounts are considered.

5. Waiver of pre-emption rights

It was proposed from the chair as a special resolution:

SPECIAL RESOLUTION

That the directors be and are hereby empowered, pursuant to the Companies Act 1985, section 95(1), to allot equity securities (as defined in section 94(2) of that Act) up to an aggregate nominal value of £1,000,000, this power to expire on the date of the next annual general meeting of the Company.

Miss Robinson proposed and Mr Smith seconded an amendment to delete the figure of £1,000,000 and substitute £200,000. The Chairman reminded the meeting that this was a special resolution and 21 clear days' notice had to be given of the actual wording of the resolution. It was therefore not possible to accept an amendment since proper notice of the substantive motion would not have been given.

Miss Robinson then proposed an adjournment for one month to enable fresh notice to be given. On a show of hands 7 members voted for and 25 against. The Chairman declared the motion to adjourn was lost.

After further discussion the Chairman put the special resolution to the vote and on a show of hands 21 members voted for the resolution and 11 members against, with several abstentions. The Chairman reminded the meeting that a special resolution required a three-fourths majority of the members voting and accordingly he must declare the resolution lost on the show of hands.

The Chairman thereupon demanded a poll and announced that it would be taken immediately. Mr Smith, dissenting shareholder, Mr Stone, auditor, and

Mr White, director, having been appointed scrutineers and voting papers having been distributed by stewards, the Chairman declared the meeting adjourned for one hour to allow the voting papers to be checked and counted. He asked members, as they left the room, to place their voting papers in the box provided near the door.

The meeting resumed at [*time*] when the Secretary, at the request of the Chairman, read the scrutineers' report which showed that 3,256,850 votes had been cast for the special resolution with 450, 750 votes against. The Chairman accordingly declared the special resolution carried by the necessary three-fourths majority.

6. Conclusion

Miss T. V. Robinson said that while she had disagreed with the Chairman on a number of points she had every admiration for the way he had conducted a difficult meeting and she would therefore like to propose a vote of thanks to the Chairman for his conduct of the meeting and to the Directors for another year's successful trading. This was carried with acclamation.

The Chairman thanked Miss Robinson and the members present and invited them to join him in refreshments which would be served in an adjoining room. This would provide an opportunity for members to meet directors and the Company's officers in a less formal atmosphere.

He then declared the meeting closed.

APPENDIX K

Specimen form of proxy

TYPICAL COMPANY p.l.c.

PROXY

Annual General Meeting, 1st December 1986

I/We (block capitals, please) ....
of ....[*address*]
being a member of Typical Company p.l.c., hereby appoint the Chairman of the meeting or ....(Note 2)
to vote for me/us at the above meeting and any adjournment thereof.

I instruct my proxy to vote as indicated by 'X' in the boxes below. On procedural resolutions or where no indication is given, my proxy may vote at his discretion.

Resolutions	*For*	*Against*
1. To receive the report and accounts	☐	☐
2. To declare a dividend	☐	☐
3. To elect (or re-elect) directors:		
3.1. Mr A. B. Black	☐	☐
3.2. Mrs E. F. Green	☐	☐
3.3. Mr L. M. White	☐	☐
4. To reappoint the auditors and (authorise the directors to) fix their remuneration	☐	☐
5. Special resolution to exclude equity pre-emption rights	☐	☐

Signed this .... day of November 1986

.... *Signature*

Notes

1. This form must be signed in the case of an individual shareholder by the appointer. A corporation may either execute it under common seal or sign by attorney or duly authorised officer of the corporation.
2. To appoint some person other than the Chairman, please make the necessary deletion, initial it and insert the name of the person you appoint. A proxy need not be a member of the Company but must attend the meeting to vote for you.
3. To be effective this proxy must reach the address shown overleaf not less than 48 hours before the time fixed to commence the meeting or any adjournment.
4. In the case of joint holders the vote of the senior will be accepted to the exclusion of the votes of others, seniority being determined by the order in which names appear on the register.
5. You may revoke this proxy by attending the meeting and voting in person.

APPENDIX L

Draft resolutions for general meetings

(See also Appendix J.)

To increase authorised capital (ordinary resolution)

That the share capital of the company be increased to [*amount*] divided into [*number*] preference shares of £1 each and [*number*] ordinary shares of 25p each by the creation of [*number*] new ordinary shares of 25p each to rank *pari passu* in all respects with the existing issued ordinary shares in the company.

To reduce capital (special resolution)

That, subject to the sanction of the court, the capital of the Company be reduced from £.......... in shares of £1 each to £.......... in shares of 25p each by the cancellation of capital to the extent of £.......... not represented by available assets and by reducing the nominal value of each share to 25p.

To capitalise reserves (ordinary resolution)

That £.......... from the company's share premium account and a further £.......... from the company's general reserves be capitalised and applied in paying up in full at par [*number*] (ordinary) shares of 25p each to be allotted as fully paid to the (ordinary) shareholders of the company in proportion as nearly as may be to their holdings at the close of business on [*date*].

To change name (special resolution)

That the name of the company be changed to '........... Limited'.

To alter objects (special resolution)

That clause 3 of the memorandum of association of the company be altered by the addition of the following paragraph:
'(Z) To publish books, papers and periodicals of every description and in any form and to deal in books, papers and periodicals published by others.'

To adopt new articles (special resolution)

That the document submitted to this meeting and signed for purposes of identification by the chairman thereof be and is hereby adopted as the articles of association of the company to the exclusion of all previous articles of association.

To alter articles (special resolution)

That regulation 18 of the articles of association of the company shall no longer apply but the following be substituted:
'18. The number of directors shall not be less than two.'

To remove a director (special notice)

That Mr .... be and is hereby removed from the office of director of the company.

To change auditors (special notice)

That Smith & Brown, the existing auditors of the company, be not reappointed but that Black & Blue, Chartered Accountants, be appointed auditors in their stead at remuneration to be fixed by the directors.

To waive pre-emption rights (special resolution)

(See Appendix J.)

APPENDIX M

Draft resolutions for board meetings

To appoint an additional director

That Mr .... be and is hereby appointed an additional director of the company.

To allot shares

The secretary laid before the meeting a schedule of share applications and reported that in all cases the money payable on application had been received. It was Resolved that [*number*] new (ordinary) shares of (25p) each in the company be allotted (fully paid) according to the schedule submitted to his meeting and signed for purposes of identification by the chairman thereof, so that each person named therein be allotted the number of shares set against his name.

To make a call

That a call of ... pence per share be made on all members [*or* on the holders of (ordinary) shares numbered ...... to ...... inclusive] payable not later than [*date*] at .... Bank p.l.c. at [*address of branch*].

To forfeit shares

That [*name*], the registered holder of [*number*] (ordinary) shares of (£1) each numbered ...... to ...... inclusive in the company, having failed to pay the call (instalment) due on [*date*] and not having complied with the notice served on him by recorded delivery post on [*date*], the said shares be and are hereby forfeited.

To declare an interim dividend

That an interim dividend of ... pence per share be paid on [*date*] on the (ordinary) shares of the company for the year ending (ended) [*date*] to shareholders registered at the close of business on [*date*].

To call a general meeting

That an extraordinary general meeting [*or* the annual general meeting] of the company be held at [*place*] on [*date*] commencing at [*time*] and that the secretary be and is hereby authorised to make all necessary arrangements.

To adopt (new) common seal

That the seal, an impression of which appears in the margin of this minute book, be and is hereby adopted as the Common Seal of the company (to the exclusion of every earlier seal, and the secretary is hereby authorised and instructed to arrange the destruction of the die and counterpart of every such earlier seal).

Note: This minute should be typed with a wider margin at the open edge of the minute book so that, when the seal is impressed alongside the minute, neither obliterates the other.

To appoint a managing director

That Mr . . . . be and is hereby appointed managing director of the company at a salary of £ . . . . per annum with effect from [*date*].

That Mr . . . . be entitled, in addition to his salary, to [*details of other emoluments*].

That Mr . . . ., as managing director, be and is hereby empowered to exercise all or any of the powers of the directors (including the power to delegate) except that he shall not contravene, countermand or act inconsistently with any specific instruction or decision of the directors and shall not without the specific authority of the board of directors:

1. Appoint any person to be a director, secretary or auditor of the company or appoint any person to any office with emoluments at a rate exceeding £ . . . . per annum.
2. Incur capital expenditure in excess of £ . . . . in any one accounting period or exceeding £ . . . . on any one item or any group of related items.
3. . . ., etc., etc.

To appoint a committee of the board

That Mr . . . ., Miss . . . ., Mr . . . . and Mr . . . . be and are hereby constituted a committee of the directors (any three to form a quorum) to investigate [*subject-matter*] and to take such action on behalf of the board as they deem necessary [*or* to recommend to this board of directors not later than [*date*] the action they consider necessary].

The said committee shall have power to co-opt to membership of the committee not more than [*number*] persons (who need not be directors) *but so that the number of non-directors on the committee shall at all times be less than half the total membership thereof and so that no decision of the committee shall be effective unless a majority of the members of the committee present are directors.

* These restrictions are required by Stock Exchange regulations for a company whose shares are 'listed'.

Subject thereto and to the articles of association of the company the committee shall regulate its proceedings as it thinks fit.

Directors' declaration of interest

General declaration of interests

Mr ...., a director of the company, gave written notice that he was a member of and therefore had a pecuniary interest in any contract made with any of the following companies:

.... Limited
.... Limited
.... Limited

Alternative for specific contract

Before discussion of this matter Mr .... informed the board that in the event of the company entering into the proposed contract he would be entitled to receive from the proposed supplier a commission of 5% on the contract price and he declared an interest in the contract accordingly.

Representative at meetings of other companies

That Mr ...., or in his absence Mr ...., be and is hereby appointed the company's representative under section 375 of the Companies Act 1985 to attend and vote for and in the name of the company at any general meeting of any company in which the company holds shares and at any creditors' meeting of any other company of which this company is a creditor, with authority to exercise all powers of the company at such meeting or any adjournment thereof.

APPENDIX N

Special resolution: layout for filing

No. . . . .(*a*)

THE COMPANIES ACTS 1948 to 1980 (*b*)

THE COMPANIES ACT 1985 (*c*)

COMPANY LIMITED BY SHARES

. . . . p.l.c. (*d*)

At an Extraordinary [*or* the Annual] General Meeting of . . . . p.l.c. held at [*place*] on [*date*] the following resolution was passed as a Special Resolution: (*e*)

SPECIAL RESOLUTION (*e*)

[*Name, printed*]

Secretary (*f*)

Notes

(*a*) Company number, as shown on certificate of incorporation.
(*b*) The Act(s) under which the company was formed.
(*c*) The Act(s) under which the change was made.
(*d*) If the name is to be changed, the *old* name appears here.
(*e*) For an increase in authorised capital substitute 'Ordinary Resolution'.
(*f*) If necessary, substitute 'Director'.

Index